Faith, Hope,
& Connection

A 30-Day Devotional for Adoptive and Foster Parents

Edited by Melissa Corkum & Lisa Qualls

Editors: Melissa Corkum and Lisa Qualls

Copy Editor: Jessica Choi

Cover Design: Isaiah Qualls and Leigh Sarti

ISBN: 9781796772500

DEDICATION

To the courageous foster and adoptive parents who choose to step into children's pain and walk the long road of healing. And to Jesus, the Healer of all.

INTRODUCTION

If there's anything we know, it's that foster and adoptive parents need community. Parenting children who come to us after experiencing trauma can be a lonely journey. Most of us feel misunderstood at times and often judged by people who are not living this unique life.

This book is a gift to you from 30 authors, all foster and adoptive parents, who offer a window into their own lives and families. You'll recognize yourself time and time again in their words.

Each one encourages you to look to Jesus, the author and perfecter of our faith (Hebrews 12:2, NASB), who is always by your side as you serve and love vulnerable children.

You are not alone.

HOW TO USE THIS BOOK

Faith, Hope, & Connection: A 30-Day Devotional for Adoptive and Foster Parents contains readings for 30 days. Each reading includes a verse from the Bible corresponding with the author's thoughts. Following each day's entry, you'll find space to journal your thoughts and prayers. This book is yours to write in, cry over, or even throw across the room. We understand "big feelings."

Read this with your spouse, a friend, or even an online support group. Discussions will be rich.

ACKNOWLEDGMENTS

Thank you to the authors who trusted us with their words and let us share them with you. You will find a brief bio for each contributor in the back pages.

Thank you to Jessica Choi for sharp copyediting. You made this a far better book.

Thank you to Leigh Sarti and Isaiah Qualls for designing the cover.

You are good parents, doing good work, often in hard circumstances. We're here for you.

Melissa Corkum & Lisa Qualls

The Adoption Connection
www.theadoptionconnection.com

Together with:

The Refresh Conference
Sponsored by Overlake Christian Church
www.therefreshconference.org

The Refresh Conference is an annual two-day conference in Redmond, WA for foster and adoptive parents and caregivers.

For bulk orders, please email us at
email@theadoptionconnection.com.

DAY 1

*For now we see only a reflection as in a mirror; then we
shall see face to face. Now I know in part; then I shall
know fully, even as I am fully known.*
1 Corinthians 13:12, NIV

There was a time in my parenting career that I thought I had all
the answers. It was about nine years ago, and I had one child.
She was six months old and right in the sweet spot of eating well
and sleeping through the night but not yet moving. This whole
parenting thing was easy. I read the books, applied the methods,
and everything worked as it was supposed to. I had this mom
thing down.

Enter crawling and tantrumming and more children, and I was
knocked right off my self-created-and-occupied pedestal. Enter
foster care and adoption, and the fact that there was ever a
pedestal, to begin with, is laughable.

I don't know about you, but I spend the majority of my days
confused. *Where's the "how to" for saying goodbye to one of your children?
What's the method for when your preschooler has a hallucination? Where's
that manual about answering your adopted child's questions about her past?*

And these practical questions? They pale in comparison to the
deeper, heavier questions of my heart. *Whatever happened to the
little boy who was in my home, whom I loved and who left? Why would the
little girl, the one we were willing to adopt, come into our family, only for her
to be moved and bounced from home to home? Will we ever be "enough" for
our adopted children, will they ever feel like they belong, ever feel fully at
home in our family? Will the behaviors and the chaos and the storm ever
pass?*

You see, I don't just struggle through the "how" questions, I
struggle through the "why" questions and the "what if" ones.
"How" questions have answers sought in books, found in
community. The "whys" and "what ifs," feel as though they're

2

cried into the darkness with nobody listening and no one to answer.

But my questions aren't ever spoken into the void. In the seeming darkness, *He* is there, shrouded in light. The one who knows everything, who searches my heart and tests my mind, who discerns my thoughts from afar (1 John 3:20, Jeremiah 17:10, Psalm 139:2, paraphrased). He hears and He listens and He knew before I even asked anyway. My questions *do* have a recipient: God in heaven above.

I feel like I should know better than to question God. *I know* what He says about Himself in His Word. He is sovereign, He is good, He's the One writing each of my days in His book (Isaiah 46:9-10, Psalm 100:5, Psalm 139:16, paraphrased). *I know* what I've experienced of Him in the past. He is faithful, He keeps His promises, He's always worked everything for my good (2 Timothy 2:13, 2 Corinthians 1:20, Romans 8:28, paraphrased). *How could I be so faithless as to question him?*

But my questions . . . they aren't accusations, they're not hopeless charges against the character or goodness of God. They're the cry of a daughter to her Father. They're the faith-filled pleas of, "I believe. Help my unbelief," (Mark 9:24). And they're an acknowledgment that, one day, I will be with Him. And He will answer. And it will all make sense.

My questions, unspoken in silent spaces or cried out violently in desperation, hang patiently in queue until that time when they will actually be asked and answered. One day, on *that* day, I will be with my Father, I will finally see Him as He truly is, and He will wipe the tears from my eyes. I will ask Him, question Him, invite Him to tell the full story of what He was working together all along. And as I stand face to face with Him, I will finally, fully know (2 Corinthians 5:10, 1 John 3:2, Revelation 21:4, 1 Corinthians 13:12, paraphrased).

This life—it can be confusing, frightening, perplexing. I only know in part, only see a mirror-like reflection. My questions, here and now, remain unanswered. But I ask them just the same. I cry them out—in faith to the God who's listening—knowing that one day, I will fully know the answers. And I will worship Him for them.

Jamie C. Finn

_____

_____

_____

_____

_____

_____

_____

_____

_____

_____

_____

_____

_____

DAY 2

*He considered that God was able even to raise him from
the dead . . .*
Hebrews 11:19, ESV

When God told Abraham to sacrifice Isaac, He was telling him
to put to death the very son he had received as a promise.
Abraham must have wondered how this call to death could
possibly have been a part of God's plan to bless all the nations
through Isaac. Isn't it the same with us? We find ourselves
wondering how the promises of God are being fulfilled in light
of our current troubles and hardships? How can this pain and
struggle, grief and loss, brokenness and death we are surrounded
by be a part of His plan for us and our kids?

In the narrative, we don't read that Abraham argued with God
or that he attempted to negotiate around it. Instead, we see
Abraham's willing obedience to walk the long and dreadful road
up Mount Moriah, where he had been called to sacrifice his son.

Not unlike the journey of adoption, his journey must have been
full of moments where he felt confusion, anger, and sadness.
Certainly, this was not his idea of the promised road down
which he thought he would be traveling. Like years of foster
parenting, the fear, fatigue, and frustration may have left
Abraham feeling weak, weary, and worn. Yet, what enabled him
to keep putting one foot in front of the other as he climbed that
mountain? What encouraged him to willingly continue on such a
hard journey of sacrifice that he believed was ultimately going to
end in the death of his son?

The writer of Hebrews helps us understand, as he points out
that Abraham, " . . . considered that God was able to even raise
[that son] from the dead."

We are not sure about you, but honestly, this is all that we have
had to hold on to at times. It is the only hope that has gotten us

through the darkest of days . . . God is able to raise from the dead.

When all we can see is a road that looks nothing like the one we thought He had promised . . . when the journey is hard, and we have uttered every prayer, exhausted every resource, and cried out for answers that haven't come . . . when we don't understand what God is doing because it looks like a broken mess of sacrifice and death that can't possibly be a part of the plan . . .

It is then, like Abraham, in faith, we must turn and consider who God is and what He is able to do:

We consider that God is able to heal hurts.

We consider that God is able to mend fractured souls.

We consider that God is able to bind up broken hearts.

We consider that God is able to calm fearful thoughts.

We consider that God is able to redeem what has been lost or stolen.

We consider that God is able to restore wounded hearts and refresh weary spirits.

We consider that He, alone, can raise what is dead inside both us and our children.

Lord, today, may we not grow weary or give up, but give us the faith to keep on, willingly and steadily, climbing this mountain, holding on to the hope that You are able.

And let us not grow weary of doing good, for in due season we will reap, if we do not give up. (Galations 6:9, ESV)

Jeff and Jen Summers

DAY 3

Anyone who listens to the word but does not do what it says is like a man who looks at his face in a mirror and after looking at himself, goes away and immediately forgets what he looks like. But the man who looks intently in the perfect law that gives freedom, and continues to do this, not forgetting what he has heard, but doing it— they will be blessed in what they do.
James 1:23-25, NIV

The Franciscan Priest, Fr. Richard Rohr, tell us, "We need to 'wipe the mirror' of our minds and hearts in order to see what's there without our distortions, or even our explanations—not what we're afraid is there, nor what we wish were there, but what is actually there. That is what a true mirror does and thus offers "perfect freedom," as referenced above in James 1:23-25.

In this same passage from this small book entitled *Just This: Prompts and Practices for Contemplation*, he says, "It requires us to stand at a distance from ourselves and listen and look with calm, nonjudgmental objectivity. Otherwise, we do not have thoughts and feelings, the thoughts and feelings have us!"[1]

As I read this, a light bulb went on in my head about my own life. I realized that when I adopted children from hard places, it somehow became a mirror into my own childhood. Before I faced the issues of loss, abuse, abandonment and other woundings my children brought into our home, I had not fully recognized so many of those issues that were still hiding in the shadows of my own childhood. I had looked at myself in the mirror and had forgotten what I looked like as a child.

As we started delving deep into the hard life circumstances of our wounded children, I found myself looking into some of the

---

[1] Rohr, Richard. *Just this: Prompts and practices for contemplation*. London: SPCK, Society for Promoting Christian Knowledge, 2018.

10

hard life circumstances of my own childhood. As my children entered therapy, so did I. Had I known then what I know now about parenting children from "hard places," I certainly would have addressed these childhood issues of my own before I brought my children home. But as I began to look into that mirror, I learned some significant things about my life that helped me better understand my children and the issues they brought with them.

I had a wonderful family who loved me deeply and did everything they knew to do to protect me and keep me safe. Unfortunately, as so often happens, I was not safe with people outside of our family, and I was forced to carry the shame and fear that comes from abuse. My family was well known in our community, and my father was a pastor, so I was taught from an early age to "not tell everything I knew." Unfortunately, I didn't feel safe to tell the horrific things that happened to me and buried them deep within.

As a result, I was an anxious child who worked too hard to please everyone and care for the needs of everyone but myself, somehow hoping that this would keep me safe and my secrets and family protected. I was "looking through a glass darkly" and not able to see the perfect freedom that the law of Christ could bring.

As I consider the deep wounds of my children, I have learned through my journey that we must help them see a true reflection of who they are in the mirror. That God's perfect love brings them freedom from their past and hope for their future. We can't offer them that hope if we don't first help them see themselves clearly in their mirror . . . and see them as God sees them.

To feel fully loved, we must feel fully known. As our children learn to know themselves and their stories, they will look into the mirror and remember the pain and the sorrow, but they will also learn the freedom that the truth can bring. "You will know the truth and the truth will set you free." (John 8:32, CSB)

I think our children act out because they are afraid that the real reflection of their story is too much for us to bear. They are afraid that if we know the truth of their hard lives, it will be more than any of us can carry. They act out because their "thoughts and feelings" have them, instead of them owning their thoughts and feelings.

To show our children the truth of God's perfect love, we must give them the perfect freedom to wipe the mirror, see clearly the truth of their story, and stand close as they remember. Then, we can remind them how loved they are by us and by God, no matter what their story holds.

Kathleen Hamer

_____

_____

_____

_____

_____

_____

_____

_____

_____

_____

DAY 4

The poor and homeless are desperate for water, their tongues parched and no water to be found. But I'm there to be found, I'm there for them, and I, God of Israel, will not leave them thirsty.
Isaiah 41:17, MSG

Normally, book club was a highlight of my month, well at least a bright spot of adult conversation on my otherwise child-focused calendar. But then life happened in a super big way. The kind of life that lifts you off your feet and dumps you upside down in the middle of a desert, seemingly devoid of any sort of help, nourishment, or rest.

After living through several months in that desert, reading "just for fun" wasn't particularly high on my to-do list. Funny how quickly worry and fear can crowd out any sort of hope or joy if we let them. In fact, if left to fester, both will merge into one giant monster that beats us up and leaves us a mere shell of ourselves.

So I didn't even read the book. I just went to the meeting to get out of the house. After six months of the aforementioned "life," I was feeling the effects of stress. I'd lost weight because all food tasted like nothing, stopped socializing with anyone, and spent hours staring into space, mentally writing the worst possible ending to our story.

Only the host, a faithful friend, and one other woman who was new to our book club showed up on this particular evening. After exchanging pleasantries, we made small talk for just a few minutes before it came up. "How is your daughter?" my good friend gently questioned.

I gave the same response I'd been giving for months, "I honestly have no idea."

She waited briefly before probing further, "And how are you?" For some reason—I don't know if it was the way she said it or just the day I'd had—the question felt like the first real invitation I'd had in a while, and something spilled over inside me. Instead of giving my normal "fine" that evening, the floodgates opened.

"How am I? How am I, really? I'm exhausted. Depressed. Scared. And you know what else? I'm angry. I've been begging God to give me someone to walk with through this ordeal. I want to know that another parent has been through this and survived. I want someone who can say, 'I understand,' but really mean it. And yet, here I am. Still walking this road alone."

Silence followed that diatribe, all except for the sounds of my pain.

"God can handle your anger. Have you told him how you feel?" my wise friend prompted.

"Ha! That's the ironic part. Because I've been talking to God a whole lot more these past few months. He's pretty much the only one I *can* talk to about it." I told her.

"So then, maybe that's His point? You're not alone, Wendy. Maybe He hasn't brought you another mom to share your pain because He wants you to share it with Him? And perhaps He wants you to feel this—really feel this—so you can walk with others later."

I stopped crying and stared at her. One part of me was saying, "Duh!" all while the other part—my human, selfish flesh— wanted to scream at the thought of being alone, only with God.

I was craving another mom, just like me, with whom I could commiserate. I wanted someone like that for two reasons. First, the turmoil in our lives made me feel like a failure. I thought if I could see someone else who'd been through a similar experience, I wouldn't feel *so* broken and *so* alone. Second, I needed to see that my current circumstances weren't insurmountable.

15

If that weren't enough, I was also mourning the fact that I couldn't fix it myself, that things weren't going according to my plan. I was carrying a pretty heavy load.

And throughout it all,

God was saying . . . *wait.*

Be patient, my child.
I love you and your family more than you can comprehend.
I have not left you, nor will I ever.
I will use this for my glory.
Your pain will not be wasted.
You are strong; you are capable with me as your guide.
And if you let me, I'll carry your load.

Wendy Willard

_____

_____

_____

_____

_____

_____

_____

_____

_____

DAY 5

When Jesus saw her weeping . . .
he was deeply moved in spirit and troubled.
John 11:33, NIV

It's a sweltering one million degrees as I sit in the back of a Land Rover on a crowded Liberian street. There are people everywhere, all staring at the white woman in the back of the car, holding a terrified and screaming Liberian two-year-old. The other adoptive moms with me encourage me to hold my new son closely and whisper truths to him. I do so. He bites me on the shoulder as hard as he can. The tears stream as the stares from those walking amongst the cars on this busy road continue.

"You shouldn't have to teach a child to love his mother." My despairing thoughts drip into my soul, like the tears streaming down my face. Both of us are scared. Both of us strangers to the other. Yet, here was my gift, the one I had longed for and prayed over. "Was it really supposed to be this hard?" I thought to myself. I thought miracles would *feel* better. I had naïve visions of my new son leaping into my arms, thrilled with the prospect of a new mommy.

But adoption isn't just miracles and love. It's also deep pain, loss, confusion, and more. Does the pain negate the miracle? Does the love negate the loss?

In a word: no.

They coexist. The love and amazement that I was sitting in a car in my long-dreamed-of-Africa while holding this boy who had crawled into my heart at first sight of his photo months before **coexisted** with the pain of realizing my son was scared, and I didn't know how to comfort him because I was, in fact, a stranger. Both sets of emotions as equally present as the other. Neither driving the other away in their intensity. Both begging for attention.

And it is here that I find Jesus.

John 11 recounts the story of Lazarus and Jesus. The chapter begins by telling us how much Jesus loved Lazarus and his sisters, Mary and Martha. Yet, when Jesus was called upon to come heal Lazarus in his time of need, He stays away and lets Lazarus die. Jesus, while still loving all three of them, has plans to resurrect Lazarus from the dead. Hands down, in my opinion, the best miracle of the Bible. But . . . one that was paved in a path of pain. A path of pain that Jesus does not deny.

Mary and Martha feel the weight of Jesus's absence, and Martha meets Him before He's even entered their town. She starts with her questions and frustrations. "If you had been here, this wouldn't have happened." I can hear the desperation in her voice. Yet, she's not afraid to share her questions with Jesus. She knows somehow that He can handle the voicing of her pain, a realization I wish so many of us could share. If only we, too, could know Jesus is safe enough to hold space for both our belief and our questions. "This didn't have to happen. This world shouldn't be this way. If only God had stopped the pain." I hear it often in the cries of my foster and adoptive friends. We weep. We question. We mourn. Yet, all too often, we carry shame for even considering these questions, rarely brave enough to voice them like Martha.

Yet even here, Martha is not only her doubts. For doubts are just a part of her story. She also holds in her heart still a tiny glimmer of hope. "Even now, God will give you whatever you ask," she seems to plead without even knowing what she's asking for or saying. The doubt. The hope. The belief. The questions. All coexisting in Martha's heart. And in mine, so often as well.

Next, they meet up with Mary. John 11:33 (NIV) says, "When Jesus saw her weeping . . . he was deeply moved in spirit and troubled."

When He saw their pain, He moved toward it. He asked to come along to the tomb. And there, in the very spot He knew would bring joy and laughter and great rejoicing, He chose first to weep with those He loved. He didn't say, "Stop your crying. Don't you know I'm going to raise him from the dead." He didn't shush them and tell them about the resurrection to come and how they would see each other again—with a wink, knowing that moment would actually be just a few minutes away.

Nope.

Jesus wept.

He entered their pain, and He wept with them. He allowed for the pain, knowing that a miracle was still coming. He honored their pain with His presence, His patience, and His very own tears.

And then . . . then He called Lazarus out of the grave, and He brought His dear friend back to life. The miracle of all miracles. The dead brought to life.

It is here I find Jesus. In the story of Lazarus and His gentleness with Mary and Martha and in my own story. I find Him in the back of a Land Rover in the middle of a hot African day. I believe on that day, He too was weeping with me. Weeping for all my son had experienced. Weeping for a naïve little mama who just wanted to comfort her long-awaited son. Weeping for all of the grief and loss and confusion. All the while holding space right there for the joy of prayers answered, miracles come, and for what He knew lay ahead of us.

He knew in that moment He would knit our hearts together as mother and son. He also knew how He would use that pain to give me a passion for African mamas across that very same continent. He knew, and yet I believe He wept with us. He held space for all that was and all that was to come. Denying none of it. Honoring all of it as sacred.

20

He weeps with you too. He weeps with you and rejoices with you and knows that very, very often, both emotions are coexisting. He doesn't ask us to deny one and sink into the other. He simply shows up at the grave and the resurrection alike, knowing both are sacred.

May we find Him there. In the coexistence of both grief and gratitude. The fullness of our stories and our emotions. The sacredness of the both/and.

Brandi Lea

_____

_____

_____

_____

_____

_____

_____

_____

_____

_____

_____

DAY 6

*Be strong and courageous; don't be terrified or afraid of
them. For it is the Lord your God who goes with you;
He will not leave you or forsake you.*
Deuteronomy 31:6, CSB

Love. It's what our adopted and foster kiddos need.
Wholehearted, unconditional love.

They have come to us with loss. An incredible loss. The loss of
their primary attachment. And because of that loss, it can be
hard for them to trust that kind of love we have for them. They
lost the very person who was supposed to take care of them.
Supposed to stay with them. Supposed to keep them safe.

It's now up to us, as their adoptive or foster parents, to show to
them, over and over again, that they are worthy of that love.
That they can trust that love. That they are safe in that love.
That no matter how bumpy, no matter how strong the
pushbacks, we will be there for them. No. Matter. What.

The road is bumpy at times. Rocky, winding, twisty, and
unpredictable. We can be filled with doubts and what ifs. What
if it isn't enough? What if I'm not enough? What if my child
doesn't heal? What if my child doesn't attach? What if I'm not
the right mom for this child? What if I'm making things worse?

When things get really hard, which they certainly can, we can
feel like a bad parent. When a child is hurting, we see those
pushback behaviors. The ones to push us back. The ones to
keep us away. The ones to protect their own fears. And the truth
is, those behaviors can be hard. Really hard. They can be ugly.
Really ugly. Yet, they work. We pull back.

We may struggle to even like, let alone love our child. And then
we don't feel like a good parent at all. When those doubts, what
ifs, and regrets creep in, that's when we can rest in that same,

unconditional, no-matter-what love. The Lord goes with us. He will not forsake us. No. Matter. What.

In the challenging times. In the good times. In the heartbreaking times. In the hopeful, happy times. He is there for us. No matter what!

Wow, isn't that powerful? Isn't that comforting?

Even in the hardest of times, be assured that you are not alone. Rest assured that you will be given the strength you need to forge ahead on this journey. The Lord goes with you every step of the way. No matter what!

We need to send that same message to our kiddos. In the challenging times. In the good times. In the heartbreaking times. In the hopeful, happy times. "I am there for you. No matter what!"

And with time and consistency, our children will begin to trust that love. To rest in that love. To feel safe in that love. To be comforted by that love. To hopefully believe, deep in their core, that they deserve that kind of love. That they are worthy of that kind of love.

To know that we will be with them, every step of the way. No matter what!

Stacy Manning

_____

_____

_____

_____

_____

DAY 7

And I will give you treasures hidden in the darkness—
secret riches. I will do this so you may know that I am the
Lord, the God of Israel, the one who calls you by name.
Isaiah 45:3, NLT

There are days when parenting children with trauma histories can feel dark and lonely.

The suffering our children have and continue to endure is a suffering we carry with them. How many days on your journey have you wondered where God was and whether the dark days would subside?

Doing your best to connect with them when they've flipped their lid, being patient when they've triggered you, trying to not feel like a failure because attachment feels nonexistent can make the most well-intentioned, loving parents wonder if they can make it through the journey. There are no guarantees and no road map, which can create an uncertainty requiring us to simply trust God in the dark.

Barbara Brown Taylor wrote in her book *Learning to Walk in the Dark*, "The God of Moses is holy, offering no seat belts or other safety features to those who wish to climb the mountain and enter the dark cloud of divine presence. Those who go assume all risk and give up all claim to reward. Those who return say the dazzling dark inside the cloud is reward enough."[2]

After eight years of parenting adopted children, I've had numerous dark days, and the last thing I often felt was safe or on the right course. The mountain seemed too steep, and I did not feel equipped for the journey. As I look back, I see how focused I was on my children's actions. What I see more clearly

---

[2] Taylor, Barbara Brown. *Learning to Walk in the Dark*. Canterbury Press Norwich, 2014.

is I needed to focus more on my own actions; not with my children but with God.

I saw the dark as evil and the enemy's dwelling to make me doubt the call of parenting kids with trauma. I did not see the dark cloud as an opportunity to sit in the divine presence with the God who knows the depths of my being better than I do. I was simply trying to survive.

What I failed to realize is sitting in God's presence was the best answer to feeling unsafe and lonely. The dark cloud was not encompassing failure but the compassion and safety of God filling my broken heart with his love and mercy.

Are you in the dark right now? Close your eyes, breathe deep, and tell God you are ready to sit with Him. Ask Him to breathe His truth into your heart. Ask Him to hold you in His tender mercies and fill you with His love. You are His daughter/son whom He wants to give treasures, and He knows you by name.

Tara Bradford

DAY 8

I said, "LORD, the God of the heavens, the great and awe-inspiring God who keeps his gracious covenant with those who love him and keep his commands, let your eyes be open and your ears be attentive to hear your servant's prayer that I now pray to you day and night for your servants, the Israelites."
Nehemiah 1:5-6a, CSB

Adoptive and foster families often find themselves barely functioning and just trying to survive when caring for children with hard behaviors. For a lot of adoptive families, trauma has left a trail of devastation not unlike what Nehemiah found when he returned to Jerusalem.

The parallel of rebuilding something after (and even during) a period of crisis and brokenness is not lost on me.

But just like the temple was rebuilt, so can we rebuild our hearts and our families.

Grieve.

When I heard these words, I sat down and wept. I mourned for a number of days, fasting and praying before the God of the heavens. (Nehemiah 1:4, CSB)

You are not crazy. You are not alone. And what your family has lost is real. Sometimes, it can feel overwhelming to consider the cost you've paid for parenting a child from a hard place. But trust me. There is hope. This season will not last forever. My experience was I couldn't move forward until I accepted the state of our family and grieved it properly.

Pray.

I said, "LORD, the God of the heavens, the great and awe-inspiring God who keeps his gracious covenant with those who love him and keep his commands, let your eyes be open and your ears be attentive to hear your servant's prayer that I now pray to you day and night for your servants, the Israelites." (Nehemiah 1:5-6a, CSB)

Understanding our kids' behaviors and having connected parenting tools are imperative in this journey, but really, healing is a God-sized job. It's a job for the One who created not just our kids but our whole world. No one understands like He does. Pray day and night (and all the moments in between) for your family as Nehemiah prayed for Israel.

Change what you *can* control.

I confess the sins we have committed against you. Both I and my father's family have sinned. (Nehemiah 1:6b, CSB)

I know the word "sin" may sound harsh, and I believe you are a *good parent* doing hard but *good work*. But can we all at least agree that we're not perfect? It's so tempting to put everything we have into changing and healing our kids. Unfortunately, while sometimes we can influence them, we cannot change them. The only person we really have control over is ourselves. Take it from someone who has tried this both ways–working on yourself is hard work but way more satisfying!

Find your people.

The men of Jericho built next to Eliashib, and next to them Zaccur son of Imri built. (Nehemiah 3:2, CSB)

Throughout Nehemiah 3, we read about all the people who helped rebuild each section of the wall. They are not always easy to find, but having friends and professionals who are on your side makes all the difference in the world.

Be persistent.

When Sanballat heard that we were rebuilding the wall, he became furious. He mocked the Jews before his colleagues and the powerful men of Samaria . . . So we rebuilt the wall until the entire wall was joined together up to half its height, for the people had the will to keep working. (Nehemiah 4:1,6, CSB)

31

Parenting kids from hard places is a marathon, not a sprint. Actually, it's like running a marathon into the wind. What you're doing is *not* easy. It's going to take grit and persistence. Be persistent in both prayer *and* action.

So we prayed to our God and stationed a guard because of [the mockers] day and night. (Nehemiah 4:9, CSB)

Stay singularly focused.

I am doing important work and cannot come down. (Nehemiah 6:3, CSB)

This task we've undertaken is important. More important than all of the other pulls in life–for now. In this season, give yourself permission to sit the next meal train out and bow out of volunteering at school and church. Besides, you need to conserve your energy so you can be persistent.

Remember the truth.

Then I replied to him, 'There is nothing to these rumors you are spreading; you are inventing them in your own mind.' For they were all trying to intimidate us, saying, 'They will drop their hands from the work, and it will never be finished.' But now, my God, strengthen my hands. (Nehemiah 6:8-9, CSB)

Whether it's your own doubts or external voices bouncing around in your head, remember these three truths:

- o You are the parent your child needs.

- o With God, healing is possible.

- o You can do this!

Write the things you know to be true on index cards, and place them in strategic places. Each time you see them, you will be reminded of the truth.

Melissa Corkum

DAY 9

God is our refuge and strength, an ever-present help in trouble. Therefore we will not fear, though the earth give way and the mountains fall into the heart of the sea, though its waters roar and foam and the mountains quake with their surging. There is a river whose streams make glad the city of God, the holy place where the Most High dwells. God is within her, she will not fall; God will help her at break of day. Nations are in uproar, kingdoms fall; he lifts his voice, the earth melts. The LORD Almighty is with us; the God of Jacob is our fortress. Come and see what the LORD has done, the desolations he has brought on the earth. He makes wars cease to the ends of the earth. He breaks the bow and shatters the spear; he burns the shields with fire. **He says, "Be still, and know that I am God**; I will be exalted among the nations, I will be exalted in the earth." *The LORD Almighty is with us; the God of Jacob is our fortress.*
Psalm 46:1-11, NIV

God talks to me through pictures. Random pictures that He brings before me and then teaches me what He wants me to learn from that image. I have to say random because that is when I anticipate His voice. A perfect example is the time He woke me with the image of me skiing on Grand Lake when I haven't water-skied in about a decade. It always becomes an ongoing conversation, usually beginning with me asking, "All right, Lord, what was that about?" Over the next 24 hours, God continued to teach me the many lessons to be found on the lake—not about how to ski or jump the wake—but how to wait for the rope.

Any of you that have skied know that when you hit that water, it's not uncommon to feel totally disoriented. My time on skis is rarely "fun" because I have to be completely engaged, thinking of every shift of my weight while watching the water ahead. Parenting is a little like that for me. We often say that "trauma-informed parenting" is counterintuitive, and I would say that it's similar to balancing every move and being ready for an upcoming "do-over." As a mom to three teens who came home through infant adoption, I had no idea I would need to be so mindful of my parenting—so mindful of their history though it embedded "*only*" in the nine months before we met and in the genetic makeup of my children. But we ski, and I focus, and I fall. It is in that moment that I am thankful for the driver of the boat, and I am thankful for my flagmen.

It is always a relief when I see that flag go up—when someone "sees" me go down. The whole point of a flagman is to keep an eye on the skier and raise the flag so no other boats hit the skier who has crashed. It is reassurance to the skier that the driver knows he or she has gone down and "let go." I am certainly surrounded by other parents who have their eye on me, quick to lift the flag to remind me I am not alone as I wait, that they are alerting the driver I have gone down—though He already knows. I am reassured that they will hold that flag up until they reach me. They will check in with me and either pull me into the boat for a break—or help me get in position to "hit it" again.

Be still and know that I am God. Be still. Stop striving and know that I see you, your flagmen see you, and we are coming for you.

In the waiting for the rope, how will I respond? How will I wait? I always cringe as the boat circles wide, and I think, "Do they even see where I am? Why are they circling so far from me?" But it is then that I see the rope skipping across the water, skillfully heading in my direction. At that point, I have another choice. Do I start to swim, thinking I know better than the driver? Do I "help" Him get to me faster because I am sure I can calculate better from my vantage point? I have certainly calculated the timing, and I am sure I can reach the rope faster than He can bring it to me. Instead, I am reminded I have been here before and the driver reminds me He's got this.

Be still and know that I am God. Be still. Stop striving and know that I see you, your flagmen see you, and we are coming for you.

While I bob in the water, I have yet another choice. Will I lie there with my face to the sun, basking in the warmth, or will I begin to wonder what lies below the surface? Will I start to speculate what can "get me" while I wait for the rope? Will I watch others ski past me and wonder how they make it look so easy? Will I feel "less than" bobbing in the water waiting for the rope? The rope, I know, will come. It comes every time. I will lie back and wait.

Be still and know that I am God. Be still. Stop striving and know that I see you, your flagmen see you, and we are coming for you.

While we navigate this difficult parenting journey, much like water skiing, may we be sure to have our flagmen, and most of all, confidence in the driver of the boat. He sees us, and He is navigating the rope back to us with expertise beyond anything we can imagine. We can rest in this, tips up and our face to the sky, waiting for the next parenting adventure—ready for a do-over.

Have you crashed? Have you gone under? Do you wonder if you even still have on your skis or your swimsuit?

Lie back and wait. Be still and know that I am God. Be still. Stop striving and know that I see you, your flag men see you, and we are coming for you.

Rebecca Vahle

_____

_____

_____

_____

_____

DAY 10

But whoever would be great among you must be your servant, and whoever would be first among you must be slave of all. For even the Son of Man came not to be served but to serve, and to give his life as a ransom for many.
Mark 10:43-45, ESV

There's a "fun" mental game that I play, now that I am a mom, that I could never have imagined prior to parenthood. The game is called, "Which bodily fluid would I prefer to clean?" I've found myself asking strange questions like this while cleaning up one or more of the aforementioned fluids. In case you are wondering, I would rather deal with poop than puke. Any day. I apologize for the mental image, but I'm assuming you have all been in similar situations.

Another strange fact I've learned about myself in my parenting journey is that I am not a fan of *feet*. I have a really hard time touching any other human's feet, including my husband's or my dear children's. Unless it is the itty-bitty toes on a fresh infant, I'll pass, thank you. So it just shows the Lord's sense of humor that my youngest kiddo has a biological disposition to stinky feet. No, stinky doesn't capture it. Actually, no words can capture it—we'd need scratch and sniff pages—but all I can tell you is that by the first grade, this child's feet *stank*. Despite one or two daily baths, sprays, powders, and special shoe inserts, his little tootsies could clear a room with their foul odor. It was just a part of life, and we tried not to make a big deal of it.

The foot odor problem did frustrate me on a superficial level, and if I'm being perfectly honest, it was also another in a growing list of obstacles to our attachment to one another. My son came home from Thailand at age two, and he and I have struggled significantly in our bonding, especially in those first few years. And I wish I could tell you that I was always the mature parent, empowered to connect with my adorable little stinker no matter what, but I frequently would ask him to go wash his feet before we could sit on the couch together to read bedtime stories.

One summer night when my son was around age six, after a busy and active day of playing outside and eating a messy dinner, I was wiping his face with a warm washcloth. I was tired and weary and facing a messy kitchen to clean. I told him I was going to wash his face and his hands. Without an ounce of irony, he then kicked up his dirty, sweaty, stinky bare feet, and said, "Will you wash my feet too?" I temporarily froze. His feet were covered in specks of mud and crumbs of food and other things I couldn't immediately identify. I did not want to wash those feet. I cannot tell you how badly I did *not* want to wash them.

But in that moment, a mundane, everyday situation suddenly felt incredibly holy. I did not hear an audible voice from the Lord, but I am certain I felt the prompting of the Holy Spirit. Would I humble myself? Would I offer to trade my dignity for my son's and treat his little body with the love and kindness he deserves? Would I model selflessness for my family, or would I refuse to do a job that I felt was beneath me?

The act of washing feet is mentioned several times in Scripture. Perhaps the most significant is in John 13 when Jesus washes the feet of his disciples, much to their dismay. Peter, especially, could barely handle the Son of God lowering Himself to such a disgraceful act, usually reserved for slaves or hired help. But Jesus was clear that this act was characteristic of the type of leader He was, and the type of leader He was calling them to be.

Jesus said to them, *"Do you understand what I have done to you? You call me Teacher and Lord, and you are right, for so I am. If I then, your Lord and Teacher, have washed your feet, you also ought to wash one another's feet. For I have given you an example, that you also should do just as I have done to you."* (John 13:12-13, ESV)

To my little guy, washing his feet was just a helpful task I could do for him, one that he probably recognized I didn't do very often. But for me, washing his feet symbolized much more. It was such a small sacrifice I could make to show him I loved him. It was gentle and loving touch that he *asked* for, a rare moment with a child who didn't hold still long enough to give hugs or make eye-contact. It was a way that I could truly, genuinely serve my son and be the type of leader and the type of mother that I believe Jesus calls me to be.

So, I wetted the washcloth again, and with tears of emotion in my eyes, I washed my son's filthy feet. I don't think he understood the significance of the moment, and that's okay. Because I did. I'm so grateful for a gracious God who is patient with me as I continue to learn what it means to be a servant leader in my home.

Jen Tompkins

DAY 11

The Lord hears his people when they call to him for help.
He rescues them from all their troubles.
The Lord is close to the brokenhearted;
he rescues those whose spirits are crushed.
Psalm 34:17-18, NLT

Heartbreaking.

That's one of many words that comes to mind when I look back over the past 15 years of this journey. Heartbroken . . . crushed . . . devastated . . . lost . . . Feel free to drop any other adjective in.

I'm not heartbroken because of my children. Nor does my heartbreak mean I regret becoming a parent or choosing to care for any of the children I've cared for or adopted. I'm heartbroken for my children. I'm heartbroken for the deep loss they've experienced in their young lives. I'm heartbroken for me. I'm crushed when I think about all of the times in the past when we misunderstood our children's behaviors, mistook them for *bad kids* instead of *wounded kids*, and reacted out of our emotion.

I wish I could take back moments . . . instances . . . words spilled like sewage . . . actions out of frustration and bitterness, and so much more.

If you're anything like me, you internalize all of this stuff. You walk through these dark moments . . . losing your temper . . . misunderstanding where your child is coming from, and feeling as though your frustration over a heartbreaking journey is somehow tied to you being a bad mom or dad.

Much like me, you believe the lies you hear whispered deep in your mind. And that leads to hopelessness.

If I had a dollar for every time I felt this way, let's just say . . . beach house in Malibu!

A couple of years ago I was reading a devotional and came across this verse:

The Lord hears his people when they call to him for help.
He rescues them from all their troubles.
The Lord is close to the brokenhearted;
he rescues those whose spirits are crushed.
The righteous person faces many troubles,
but the Lord comes to the rescue each time.
For the Lord protects the bones of the righteous;
not one of them is broken!
Psalm 34:17-20, NLT

This is a Psalm written by King David when he was in the deepest of all depths of despair and agony. It was written by a man who was suffering from way more than heartbreak. He was suffering through brokenness on such a deep level that it really is hard to comprehend. I would equate it to the loss of a child, or someone you loved so much you couldn't imagine living without them.

The descriptive language used in this Psalm both fascinates and haunts me. *Troubles. Crushed. Broken.*

My friend . . . how closely do these words represent our day-to-day on the adoption journey?

But let me turn your attention to some other words we can often miss, not just in a verse like this but also in life when we are struggling to breathe . . .

Hears. Rescues. Close. Protects.

This journey is hard. Our kiddos' past trauma is devastating and can take the life out of us as we work hard to care for them through the dark storm of their past. We are exhausted, crushed, broken, and lost most days.

But the God who carved out the ocean depths and dotted the night sky with stars is close to us and our broken hearts. He's holding us in the palm of His hands. And He's holding our beautiful children. You are not hopeless. Your children are not hopeless. You are held by the creator. He protects you and your children. He rescues us when we are in despair.

The Lord is close to the brokenhearted.

Mike Berry

DAY 12

God, the Lord, is my strength; he makes my feet like the
feet of a deer, and makes me tread upon the heights.
Habakkuk 3:17-19, NRSV

Both. And.

There is a song we sing at our church baptisms. As each
individual is baptized and comes out of the water, we sing this
blessing from Zephaniah 3:17.

The Lord your God is with you,
He is mighty to save.
He will take great joy in you.
He will quiet you with his love.
He will rejoice over you with singing.
Alleluia.[3]

This is my prayer for each of you today.

Most of us enter adoption and foster care with high hopes and
dreams, which is as it should be. We dream of a better world, a
world where children are loved, valued, and nurtured. We long
for them to find healing and strength and maturity and healthy
adulthood because of being loved, valued, and nurtured. We
hope to be the instruments of healing, the messengers of hope.

This is not something to scoff at. No one begins to work for a
better world without hopes and dreams of how that will work
out.

And no one achieves those dreams without some measure of
realism, of pain, or disillusionment along the way. My own
assumptions were that if God had called us to this, then God
would also make us successful. When we got to the point where
we had to admit we did not know what to do and could no

---

[3] Composed by Nathan Stucky, Ph.D. Printed with permission.

longer manage the rage and chaos, it was such a devastating point. It was not only a recognition of our own failure to parent according to our ideals, but also a feeling of abandonment by God.

How could God call us to something and not also make it possible? Why would God ask us to do things that seemed impossible?

We cling to the passages of hope in the Bible, the promises, like the one above, sometimes not recognizing that the promise of rescue includes the reality that we will need rescuing. We will have problems. Struggling is not an indicator of abandonment. It is important to remember this.

In the midst of life not working out, in the center of failure and pain, God is still loving you, loving us. The truth is that God's love for us holds steady, even when we can't feel it . . . even when we are at our lowest points. Even when we are angry with God. Even when we feel abandoned. The Lord your God is with you. God is mighty to save. God quiets you with love. God rejoices over you with singing.

The prophet Habakkuk began his writing with a diatribe against God. The psalmists also brought their complaints against God. Job was open about his angry assessment that he did not deserve the disasters that befell him. Being honest with God about our disappointments, and even our rage at God, is biblical. God desires honesty. It isn't the end of the story.

Habakkuk and God worked through the rage and accusations, and the final words of the book are well known.

Though the fig tree does not blossom,
and no fruit is on the vines;
though the produce of the olive fails,
and the fields yield no food;
though the flock is cut off from the fold,
and there is no herd in the stalls,
yet I will rejoice in the Lord;

47

I will exult in the God of my salvation.
God, the Lord, is my strength;
he makes my feet like the feet of a deer,
and makes me tread upon the heights. (3:17-19, NRSV)

Habakkuk could not begin with this, but as he brought it honestly to God, he came to the truth. He could go through the hard things and still rejoice in God. Craig Groeschel, in his study of Habakkuk, *Hope in the Dark*, says that the very name, Habakkuk, has a dual meaning. It means to struggle, and to embrace.[4]

Both. And.

Paul also speaks of this in 2 Corinthians 4:

We are afflicted in every way, but not crushed; perplexed, but not driven to despair; persecuted, but not forsaken; struck down, but not destroyed; always carrying in the body the death of Jesus,
so that the life of Jesus may also be made visible in our bodies . . . (v.8-10)
So we do not lose heart . . . (v.16, NRSV)

I've spent a lot of time wondering about this . . . about how we are crushed, perplexed, persecuted, struck down, but do not lose heart. Truly, I have lost heart at times. Maybe you have too.

The thing I have learned is that we have to hold on to both truths.

The first truth? We are not called to ease. We are called to faithfulness, even when things turn out differently than we hoped. We are called to follow Jesus, who was obedient through all things.

---

[4] Groeschel, Craig. *Hope in the Dark: Believing God Is Good When Life Is Not*. Grand Rapids, MI: Zondervan, 2018.

The second truth? We can be honest with God about all our emotions while always being deeply and completely loved by God in ways we cannot even begin to comprehend.

Both. And.

You have not been abandoned. Struggle is not a sign of abandonment. It is a sign of engagement with God in the redemption of the world.

The Lord your God is with you.
He is mighty to save.
He will take great joy in you.
He will quiet you with his love.
He will rejoice over you with singing.
Alleluia.

So be it.

Bev Regier

_____

_____

_____

_____

_____

_____

_____

_____

DAY 13

Three times I pleaded with the Lord to take it away from me. But he said to me, "My grace is sufficient for you, for my power is made perfect in weakness." Therefore I will boast all the more gladly about my weaknesses, so that Christ's power may rest on me. That is why, for Christ's sake, I delight in weaknesses, in insults, in hardships, in persecutions, in difficulties. For when I am weak, then I am strong.
2 Corinthians 12:8-10, NIV

"Why are you so darn happy?" spewed my childhood friend during a visit we were having in her freshman dorm room. While I couldn't respond with words, all I could think was, "The joy of the LORD is my strength and the source of my nonstop positive energy. If she doesn't get it, she must have a spiritual problem. If she accepted some joy from the LORD, maybe she wouldn't be such a wet blanket."

During the next three years, hardship relentlessly struck, and I began to struggle with anxiety and sleep difficulty. I read 2 Corinthians 12 and, without studying the Scripture thoroughly, began to pray that God would replace my weakness with His strength. A few months later, when life was a bit easier, my anxiety seemed to vanish, and my sleep returned. I determined God had answered my prayer. So, for the next few years, whenever I felt weak, I continued to pray and wait for His strength to arrive and dissolve my weakness.

After caring for children and adults from hard places for years, I revisited the Scripture that had become so dear to me, and I couldn't make sense of it. I was praying for Him to take my weakness and give me His strength, but He wasn't doing it. I was weaker than I'd ever imagined being. My energy was depleted to the point where I was asking God to intervene miraculously so I could smile at my precious children when I greeted them each morning. Where was the joy that had once provided me with endless energy? I cherished my children and wanted to enjoy them, but when I woke each day, it was a challenge to see beyond the daily battle I'd have to again engage in just to keep our family safely together. I no longer recognized myself. Where was His strength?

I recently read 2 Corinthians 12 again, and, for the first time, I had a revelation. Nowhere in that passage does Paul imply that God promises to replace my weakness with strength. Rather, His strength comes in the midst of human weakness. In fact, most scholars believe Paul's thorn in his flesh was a physical ailment (such as migraine headaches) that remained chronically even though he prayed for healing. In his compromised physical state, Paul learned to boast in his weakness, acknowledging Christ's power would rest on him during those times.

Reading Scripture anew, I began to look back at times I've questioned His unwillingness to provide me with strength over the past couple of decades.

When, after ten months of relative isolation, I ventured out of the house to spend time with a friend only to return to see my car had been vandalized by a child who believed this friendship was a threat to her safety, His grace was sufficient. His power was made perfect. My weakness remained.

When I wearily woke at the crack of dawn so I could patch and paint drywall before bedtime because a traumatized child was so insecure about food that he ate a hole in his wall in the middle of the night, His grace was sufficient. His power was made perfect. My weakness remained.

When I was lying on our dining room floor in the fetal position having an anxiety attack, and my eight-year-old child had to call his dad to come home from work, His grace was sufficient. His power was made perfect. My weakness remained.

I'm a very different person today than I thought I would be when I was judgmental of my friend's moodiness in her dorm room. Then, I thought I had all the answers. Now, I know I have more questions than answers. Then, I had endless energy and mistook Scripture to mean that my positive energy was a product of my obedience. Now, I'm depleted and have to wait on God's power, praying that He'll work despite me and my brokenness. Back then, I succeeded (and even aced) any measurable task given to me. Now, I can acknowledge that my faithfulness rarely yields immediate results that anyone in the world can see. When God intervenes in our family, it's obvious that the work is His and I'm merely a spectator, constantly waiting for Him to provide.

These days, I'm reminded that if I have one defining human characteristic, it is my weakness. The good news is that in the face of my weakness, His grace is sufficient. His power is made perfect. I am still very, very weak. He is forever strong.

Nicole Pritchard

_____

_____

_____

_____

_____

_____

_____

_____

DAY 14

Love bears all things, believes all things, hopes all things,
endures all things. Love never fails.
1 Corinthians 13:7-8a, ESV

There is a popular cliché, repeated by adoptive parents and professionals alike, that "love is not enough." I understand what they intend with the phrase. Far too often, we parents enter adoption with simplistic and idealistic expectations created from ignorance and romantic wishful thinking. One common misconception is that simply bringing a child into a safe home with "loving" parents will bring healing and peace to even the most wounded child. When our unrealistic expectations fail to materialize, they spawn anger, resentment, bitterness, and despair, resulting in great harm to everyone involved.

I confess that "love is not enough" sounds compelling, especially when blindsided by the brutal consequences of complex developmental trauma. There we sit, feeling like we've been flattened by a truck in our own family room and trying to make sense of how we got to this place. We recognize the foolishness of our unrealistic expectations and understandably conclude that love being enough is a flawed and naïve concept. As reasonable as this sounds, this conclusion is mistaken.

Instead, it is our concept of love that is flawed and naïve. Let's consider what Paul has to say about love in 1 Corinthians 13, which I've paraphrased and expanded.

Love suffers through the hard, for as long as it takes, and its suffering is not focused on the hardship. Love suffers together with the one that is loved, fully attuned to their pain and fear, to ensure they don't suffer alone. Love sticks together.

Love is considerate and courteous, gentle and gracious, thoughtful and understanding, tolerant and forgiving, tenderhearted and generous. Love makes itself useful. Love meets needs.

Love doesn't dwell on what others have that it does not. Love knows that the gap between itself and others exists only because it has chosen to stand in the gap on behalf of the one it loves. Love willingly pays that price. Love sacrifices.

Love doesn't take pleasure in having what others do not. Love cares more about the unmet needs of others than the glorification of itself. It is grateful for the blessings of the moment, regardless of whether they prove to be lasting or ephemeral. Love gives.

Love does not inflate its own importance over another. Love sees the preciousness in others. Love respects.

Love never attempts to better itself by diminishing another and will willingly diminish itself to better another. Love knows that the apparent gains from selfish actions are illusory and ultimately diminish both the other and itself. Love empowers.

Love is not easily angered, because anger is an expression of fear, and love does not operate from fear. Love and fear are incompatible and cannot occupy the same space. Anger arises to hide fear, pain, sadness, and shame. Love embraces vulnerability.

Love does not keep score. Love cares nothing for what came before except where it provides understanding and compassion of what comes after. Love does not find victory in counting itself ahead of others; it counts itself ahead when it helps others find victory. Love champions.

Love never takes satisfaction from injustice visited upon another. Love knows the truth: unjust gains never satisfy. Knowing the truth frees love to act. Love is never afraid to do what is right. Love is unfettered.

Love protects in all circumstances, anticipating where protection will be needed and arranging safety before the threat arrives. Love does not protect with half measures; it puts in place protection from all sides, even from within. Love's protection bears up under the strain. Love sustains.

Love has endless faith in the one it loves. Love does not shrink back when rejected but instead leans into the discomfort, knowing that behind the hurtful defenses is a hurting person. Love believes to its core that the one it loves is worth the effort and that its efforts will not be in vain. Love trusts.

Love never loses hope. Love hopes with reckless abandon. Love dares to hope even when all seems lost. Love is tenacious.

Love endures through everything. It cannot be quenched or thwarted. Love may find its way blocked, or diverted, or obscured, but it overcomes such things because it persists through every obstacle. Love is unstoppable.

Love is the ultimate superpower. Love does not fail; cannot fail. Love's only real enemy is fear; and love, real, pure, unconditional love drives away fear. It banishes fear and forbids it to return. Love prevails.

When times are easy, there is no need for a love that endures all things or a love that suffers long. But when times get hard, when we are pushed beyond our limits, when all "feelings of love" have fled, leaving behind only our conviction to love, and we then choose to love despite all the hard. It is then that we develop the capacity to love with tenacity, to love with abandon, to love deeper and more thoroughly than we ever believed possible. Love grows best in adversity and is perfected in the crucible of the hard.

Loving this completely does not happen in isolation. We need the support of friends, relatives, doctors, therapists, coaches, mentors, and helpers.

Nor is love like this passive. Love pursues every avenue, seeks out every aid, studies, learns, experiments, and invests. Most of all, we need others who give this kind of love to us. Learning to love is hard work, but whenever I lean into the discomfort of love, I find myself more free to love.

For now, I can only claim to understand love this deep in glimpses. Before adopting, I thought I understood love, but I was mistaken; my concept of love was naïve and flawed. I now experience moments where I love with a purity and intensity that approaches the kind of love Paul described. In those moments, I see my kids experience what it feels like to live free from fear and know they are precious. I firmly believe that when we live this kind of love, then yes, absolutely, love is enough. Love never fails. Love wins.

Mark Vatsaas

_____

_____

_____

_____

_____

_____

_____

_____

_____

_____

_____

_____

_____

_____

DAY 15

Forget the former things; do not dwell on the past. See, I am doing a new thing! Now it springs up; do you not perceive it? I am making a way in the wilderness and streams in the wasteland.
Isaiah 43:19, NIV

"If I don't quit, I win," has become my life mantra. I've learned that regardless of the "too hard" things that life brings, the best thing I can do is press into my Father. I don't understand the whys behind things that happen, nor do I try to figure them out. What I do know, however, is my Father is faithful every single time to help me. Cancer and trauma have been my biggest teacher of this, as well as the ordinary and unordinary things of being a mama of nine precious jewels. My Father has not only miraculously healed our youngest jewel but also has healed things in me. These moments of my Father's healing and shifting literally happen all the time.

It was two days until our Jax's next MRI when the doctors would once again scan for cancer. I felt broken and weary, and all I wanted to do was lie in my bed and cry the day away. We were coming up on two years of Jax being cancer-free, yet all my mind could think about was the two years of fighting cancer. I felt completely overwhelmed and like my heart might break. Memories from the hospital flooded my mind, memories of the sights, the sounds, and the smells. Jax had fought cancer fiercely with there being times when the doctors told us Jax was not going to make it.

My grief over all that had been lost during the last several years felt unleashed.

   o   my grief that our youngest jewel could no longer see, as cancer had taken his sight

- o my grief over how the medical trauma had changed all nine of our jewels, seven of whom already had their own trauma stories

- o my grief that five months earlier we had relocated to Arizona, leaving a blessed life in Washington behind

For days now in the quiet with my Father, I had been begging Him to lift the weariness, but nothing seemed to shift in me. In the unleashing of my grief, I felt as if I didn't have the strength to face the next scan.

On my early morning run, I experienced a new thing. I had decided to have my iTunes on shuffle, and the first song that played, I had never heard before. The words said, "Restless heart, do not grow weary . . . " My Father had messed with my iTunes and played this song just for me. The next few songs felt equally selected by my Father, and I could feel my heart beginning to shift. Then a sermon came on, a sermon I had never heard before and didn't even know was on my playlist. I tried several times to stop it, but nothing worked. I heard Isaiah 43:19, NIV: **"Forget the former things; do not dwell on the past. See, I am doing a new thing! Now it springs up; do you not perceive it? I am making a way in the wilderness and streams in the wasteland."**

My crying changed to sobbing as my Father was literally messing with my iTunes to not just minister to my heart but to heal it. In moving to Arizona, God had given me Isaiah 41:18, NIV: **"I will make rivers flow on barren heights and springs within the valleys. I will turn the desert into pools of water."** The previous weeks, I had literally been meditating and soaking my heart with Isaiah 41-42. As I ran, I heard the Holy Spirit say to be prepared to stand and be amazed at what my Father was about to do. I felt something shift, and I knew I no longer had to worry about the impending MRI, as my Father had it covered. I also heard the Holy Spirit say that my Father was going to make roads and rivers for us in the desert, and 2019 was going to be a year of my Father doing "new things" of huge "stand

and be amazed" moments. Literally, within the time frame of a four-mile run, my Father shifted things in me, and my heartfelt renewed and full of hope.

During the next several mornings of sitting with my Father, I prayed into the word He had given me for 2019. Tenderly, I heard the Holy Spirit say that I didn't have to wait until 2019, as my Father was already doing miraculous new things every single day. He reminded me of our eighth-grade daughter who, despite her insecurities over having a hand difference, went out for basketball at her new school and made the team. He reminded me of our youngest, who despite being blind, got up every day with such deep joy. He reminded me of our oldest jewel who, as a junior in high school, had sacrificially and bravely left best friends, varsity cheer, and a worship team behind. He reminded me of the recent tenderness in my middle jewel who was just now beginning to heal from our cancer journey. He reminded me of our second youngest jewel who, despite spending her first three years in an orphanage of four hundred orphan jewels, had learned how to trust. He reminded me of many new things, and I was renewed in that I didn't need to wait until 2019 for our Father to do the new and miraculous.

Every day, our Father does miraculous new things, and He invites us to not only look for them but also to expect them. Our Father does these new things whether we are in the desert of life where everything feels barren, or whether we are geographically living in the desert. Some of the new things are huge and obvious, while others are so subtle that if we aren't paying attention, we will miss them. He promises us new things and invites us to stand and be amazed and to let them heal and renew us.

Maria Hansen-Quine

DAY 16

*For His Holy Spirit speaks to us deep in our hearts and
tells us that we are God's children . . . Can anything ever
separate us from Christ's love? I am convinced that
nothing can ever separate us from His love. Death can't,
and life can't. The angels can't, and the demons can't.
Our fears for today, our worries about tomorrow, and
even the powers of hell can't keep God's love
away . . . nothing in all creation will ever be able to
separate us from the love of God that is revealed in
Christ Jesus our Lord.*
Selected from Romans 8:16-39, NLT

In the adoption journey, many a parent has experienced a
profound sense of failure if they perceive that bonding is not
happening. The truth is, adoption is a response to trauma that
occurred. Something has gone wrong. Adoption has been
chosen as the intervention and the answer. When bonding
becomes the criteria for success, an unrealistic expectation has
been placed on both the child and the parent.

Bonding is a bonus, not a prerequisite, in adoption.

It takes time and real energy to deal with trauma. Faithfulness
for the long haul is essential. Take time to consider this letter
that Bev wrote to our adopted sons about this reality:

My Dear Sons,

She was alone and afraid, just a child herself. The women of the
slum had assisted with the delivery of her baby boy just days
before. She had no family to speak of, at least not that were in a
position to shelter her from the harsh realities that shaped her
existence. Without adequate nutrition herself, she had no life-
giving nourishment to offer her tiny son. She did the only thing
she knew to do, offering her famished baby polluted, lead-laced
water mixed with sugar. At least it would briefly calm the cries
of hunger.

She knew the battle against hunger was one she would lose. She knew her son would not survive. She knew her own indentured servitude would not allow her to care for her baby. She knew that her opportunity for anything beyond what was would likely not be hers in her tiny island nation of Haiti.

She had heard of a young man in her district who was working for an American. She had heard that the American had an orphanage where her baby could be fed and cared for. She knew this was her only viable option. The survival of her baby boy depended on this. Her own survival depended on this.

~~~~~~~~~~~

Our return flight had taken us from Port-Au-Prince through Miami and then straight on to Seattle Tacoma International Airport. We were weary and ready to finally be home. You were now fourteen-months-old, stocky and well nourished. All physical signs of your precarious beginnings erased. There were, however, other symptoms pointing to the uncertainties of your first year of life. Telltale signs of lack of opportunity to bond.

You did not sleep. After several nights of trial and error, you and I settled into a fitful routine born out of exasperation. I drifted in and out of sleep on the couch with one arm dangling down into the playpen where you dozed. Every thirty minutes or so, you would open your eyes, check to see if I was still there, and then briefly doze off again. This was our arrangement, night after night, week after week, month after month. Somewhere around the one-year anniversary of our flight home, you finally became convinced of my staying power and allowed yourself to sleep peacefully. In your short little life, you had awakened to find many caregivers gone. It seems you had finally found one who wasn't leaving. Everything changed in that moment of revelation.

Years later, another of your adolescent siblings would say to me, "Everyone I have ever loved has either died or abandoned me. I will never open myself up to that again." It seems your sibling had also had a soul awakening to the indescribable emptiness of loss.

~~~~~~~~~~

Trauma and bonding are bitter enemies fighting a battle over staying power.

Trauma is the reality of being wounded by the circumstances of life. Whether the victimization of a young Haitian girl, the incarceration of a woman caught in the web of addiction, the toll of diseases of poverty, or the death of a cherished grandparent and caregiver, we have experienced the devastating fallout of trauma. It was never your fault. Trauma just is. It has been the unwelcomed and uninvited guest at the table of life from the beginning of time. Trauma affects us all. When trauma takes hold, there is no space it will not infiltrate, no sanctuary free from its grasp.

Each of us responds uniquely to the trauma we experience. Sleeplessness, hurt, anger, anxiety, confusion, control, self-loathing, and isolation can all be natural responses to the trauma in our lives. There is never a reason to feel ashamed of the emotions we are feeling. It is part of the process of grieving our losses. Grieving is necessary. Grieving is good. Walking through the grieving process breaks the fetters which hold us captive to the traumatic experiences of our past.

Your father and I have chosen to grieve with you. We have chosen to stay. We understand fully that bonding is not a prerequisite for healing. Staying power is the prerequisite for healing. Bonding happens in its own sweet time as a natural quality of healing and wholeness.

You see, there is a God who is unwavering and relentless in His staying power on behalf of each of us. His redemptive will and the indomitable spirit He has instilled in you and me give us everything necessary to triumph over the anguishing events of life. Absolutely nothing can ever separate us from God's love. No traumatic event, no anguishing reality, no loss.

Together, we have grieved. Together, we have triumphed.

Staying in this with you,

Mom

Ed and Bev McDowell

_____

_____

_____

_____

_____

_____

_____

_____

_____

_____

_____

_____

_____

DAY 17

*Train up a child in the way they should go
and when they are old they will not part from it.*
Proverbs 22:6, NIV

I used to think that this Scripture meant that if I raised my children "right," they would never get in trouble. They would never suffer. They would never make poor choices, never be unkind, never part from the Lord, never question their faith. I misunderstood. I have eight children. Two of them are grown adults, three are teens, and three are preteens. I have done everything in my power to raise them "right," and guess what? They are still human! As a matter of fact, I'm still human. Sigh. So much for perfection.

A good friend pointed out that the Scripture actually says, "Train up a child in the way they should go and when they are *old* they will not part from it." Hmmm, that got me thinking. My kids have a lot of life to live before they get old. They have a lot of choices to make, a lot of chances for failure and success. They will make good choices and not so good choices. They will feel strong and firm in their faith some days, and some days, they will feel quite empty. Isn't this the way of life?

When I read this Scripture now, I see a few more words of encouragement: "train" and "the way they should go." The Bible never implies that we are called to perfection; it calls us to point the way. Show your children how to walk this path, how to live this life, how to fall and get back up, how to succeed with grace, and how to fail with courage.

Our children will learn the way to go by following our lead.

How can we lead them well? Through connection. Our children don't learn what we believe just through Bible study, devotions, or shared prayer. They learn what direction we are going by observation.

Time: Spend time with your child. Not just at special times like during family vacations or holidays but also in the realities of life. Grocery shop with your child. Take them to visit you at your place of work. Stand beside them while they are doing chores. Work, play, and relax with your children. It is in the mundane, everyday living that our children will see our true character and, in turn, begin to piece together the parts of their own identity that will last them throughout life.

Experience: Create experiences for your child to walk in the ways of the Lord alongside you. Serve others, greet neighbors, widen your family's circle. Our desire can be to surround our children with only the good and loving and easy things of this world. Resist this urge. As your children see you interact with those who are different, their own identity will grow. As they experience your love toward others, they too will internalize the teachings of Jesus Who stood firm in His faith while loving others without question.

Honesty: Humanity is a struggle. It is for everyone. Be honest with your children when things are hard. Be open about your questions and your curiosity. Your children will doubt. They will have difficulties. They will face questions for which they have no answer. That is ok. God is ok with our uncertainty. He can handle it; He is certain about us. Our children will learn to turn to the Lord in times of doubt by watching us do the same.

Kristin Berry

_____

_____

_____

_____

DAY 18

Praise be to the God and Father of our Lord Jesus Christ,
the Father of compassion and the God of all comfort,
who comforts us in all our troubles, so that we can
comfort those in any trouble with the comfort we
ourselves receive from God.
2 Corinthians 1:3-4, NIV

I sat on the floor of my closet, sobbing into the phone. Surely, none of the children would hear me if I hid among the clothes. "Mom, this is going to be my life. From now on, I will hear the screaming every single day." I didn't question if I could do it or even how. I only expressed my belief that this would never end. It was terrifying.

We had just brought home a child whose brain was so disorganized by drugs and alcohol that emotional regulation was severely compromised. Had it been weeks or only days when I called my mom? I'm unsure now, but it felt like we'd been doing this forever, and I was tired. I didn't want anyone or anything going near my child. As soon as one little thing triggered the screaming, it would go on until exhaustion took over and a nap brought peace.

My mom's words escape me now, but I easily recall the feeling. She got it. Her experience was not like mine, but she understood me. My mom's empathy calmed and strengthened me. When we said goodbye, I returned to my children with love and comfort.

I haven't always been surrounded by empathy. Many times, I have felt alone and misunderstood. The needs of my family have often caused feelings of alienation. I have been asked to leave groups; I've lost friends; and we even moved away from a community that was judgmental and ostracizing. Some moments did cause me to question, "Can I keep doing this?"

Regardless of the intense loneliness, I never gave up. Trauma experts have shown that the reliable presence of one attuned person can strengthen our resilience. My mom has been a constant caregiver through the decade since that call. She has been available through the valleys and on the mountaintops, always an empathic presence.

There is empathy available to us all. The omnipresent Caregiver does not watch from afar, allowing us to remain alienated. He gave a piece of Himself, His own Son, to live among us and experience with us so that He may empathize. The Son did not then leave us as orphans but now lives in us through His Holy Spirit, our Comforter and Counselor. Now, we may boldly approach the Father for mercy and grace when we are in need. (Hebrews 4:14-16; John 14:18-26, NIV)

My mom has not lived close enough to always be the hands-on grandmother so many families have, but she is emotionally available. She has listened to many tears through the phone, read emails riddled with discouragement, and flown across the country to be close during crises. Her attunement did not begin with the call in the closet, but during my infancy. It was through her availability that I came to know the Father as a child, and I now pass that on to my children.

The all-day, everyday screaming has ceased. It did not become my life. Through consistent empathy, I became the attuned caregiver who regulates with my child. This child, whose brain has not healed, has a heart that can be comforted, and resilience has developed.

As a family, we are now able to empathize with others on a similar journey and offer comfort. We have since fostered many children and now support foster and adoptive families in very practical ways. We all have the ability to act as attuned caregivers.

Praise be to the God and Father of our Lord Jesus Christ, the Father of compassion and the God of all comfort, who comforts us in all our troubles, so that we can comfort those in any trouble with the comfort we ourselves receive from God. (2 Corinthians 1:3-4, NIV)

When you find yourself hiding in the closet, I encourage you to reach out to the One who understands. You have a direct line to a Caregiver who is always, always available. He has seen you, watching you grow from infancy, and heard all of your cries. He is the attuned Father, reaching to pull you out from behind the clothes. He supplies your every need and comforts you in your distress so that you can carry on. Through Him, you can keep going. Through Him, you will become the comforter.

Tereasa M. Mansfield

_____

_____

_____

_____

_____

_____

_____

_____

_____

_____

_____

DAY 19

Therefore we do not give up. Even though our outer person is being destroyed, our inner person is being renewed day by day. For our momentary light affliction is producing for us an absolutely incomparable eternal weight of glory. So we do not focus on what is seen, but on what is unseen. For what is seen is temporary, but what is unseen is eternal.
2 Corinthians 4:16-18, HCSB

Weary.

Weary. If ever a word felt loaded, it's this one, and I am thankful for it. I am thankful for a word that goes beyond simply being tired, a word that doesn't sound as exaggerated and overused as exhausted. The word, weary, nails it for me.

Merriam-Webster defines weary as:

1: exhausted in strength, endurance, vigor, or freshness

*2: expressing or characteristic of **weariness***

3: having one's patience, tolerance, or pleasure exhausted

4: wearisome.

In my journey as an adoptive sibling, I have watched as this word defined my parents for years, possibly decades, which came nowhere near the experience of profound and unexpected weariness in my own life later on as a wife, mom, ministry leader, and friend.

Weary . . . as relationships I thought were solid unravel before my eyes.

Weary . . . as I realize the books I have read about parenting, marriage, and leadership all fall short.

Weary . . . as I seek counsel and insight from "experts" that all seem to conflict and leave me with more questions than answers.

For me, the weariness led not only to a disheartened feeling but also a complete and total disorientation. If everything I thought I knew, believed, and prepared for was lacking when it came to reality, where did that leave me? I can tell you where: in a pit.

Maybe you've been there. The "Christian" books leave you feeling like a failure. Conversations leave you feeling misunderstood. Counselors make solutions sound pat and easy. Yet, nothing is coming together. It is at these times that God feels distant, the Bible feels irrelevant, and a personal relationship with this loving God seems just out of reach . . . something for other people, perhaps.

Oh friend, I have been there. Then God gently reminds me He is here. The reminder I cling to is this:

Therefore we do not give up. Even though our outer person is being destroyed, our inner person is being renewed day by day. For our momentary light affliction is producing for us an absolutely incomparable eternal weight of glory. So we do not focus on what is seen, but on what is unseen. For what is seen is temporary, but what is unseen is eternal. (2 Corinthians 4:16-18, HCSB)

We are not abandoned; none of our suffering is missed by God's watchful eye. In fact, He is not even inactive on our behalf, even though it seems that way. When I look at the absolute mess, I can't see it. It makes me exhausted . . . weary. I can't see that He is at work when I look at the behavior of my kids. I am not feeling the connection to God when I feel lonely in my own home. I am not experiencing God's nearness when I am focused on the earthly mess, but I know He is here, He sees it, He is working. This is so hard, yet so simple. It doesn't require a new counselor or another book on marriage, parenting, or trauma (while insightful, true hope does not come from this). It simply requires that I change my perspective and trust the mess to a

75

good God who is making all things new. When I change my perspective, I make way for a great exchange. In order to do this, I have to give something up. I have to give up the past . . . the things I have relied on offering false hope in exchange for God's activity on my behalf:

Forget the former things; do not dwell on the past. See, I am doing a new thing!
Now it springs up; do you not perceive it? I am making a way in the wilderness and streams in the wasteland. (Isaiah 43:18-19, NIV)

In my weariness, God has asked me for the one thing I can provide: a wasteland. I have managed to create one of those, and all I have to do now is trust that in unseen ways, He is preparing a stream of eternal significance. If that isn't a good trade-off for weariness, I don't know what is.

Jen Decker

DAY 20

"My friends, even though we have a lot of trouble and suffering, your faith makes us feel better about you. Your strong faith in the Lord is like a breath of new life."
1 Thessalonians 3:7-8, ESV

Take a breath. No . . . I mean, take a *deep* breath. Slow down. Tune in to your body. That amazingly complex body that was created by God. Now . . . take a deep breath. Feel your lungs expand as you slowly breathe in. Hold onto it . . . and slowly exhale. Now, do that five more times, and each time you do it, exhale a little more audibly through your mouth. Visually see the frustrations and angers of the day exhale out of your body and mind with each exhale.

Breath. It was with the holy breath of God that you were formed. He breathed *life* into us. Into me. Without our breath, we are dead. Nothing. A shell of what we were.

There are days, though, when the darkness and fog seem so thick around me that I just can't seem to find my way. I feel trapped. Alone. Abandoned by everyone. And desperate for help. It's almost like I just can't breathe and the thought of not knowing what to do brings me to tears.

Are you in the thick of it with your kids? I'm here, too, on this journey with you. And I feel short of breath.

I've always instantly loved my kids. But not this time. This one I honestly don't want to be around. This older child . . . and my feelings for this older child . . . are different. How can I help the other kids love and accept this child when I can't even do it myself? How can I love this child when I really just want to run away?

Attaching as a parent of an older child is *not* easy, and there is no recipe or formula for instantaneous love, attachment, or bonding. All I know is that I feel done. Like I'm empty with nothing left to give. Like I'm all dried out. Like I'm barely breathing.

But then, God shows me this:

The Lord said, "Ezekiel, son of man, can these bones come back to life?"

I replied, "Lord God, only you can answer that."

He then told me to say:

Dry bones, listen to what the Lord is saying to you, "I, the Lord God, will put breath in you, and once again you will live. I will wrap you with muscles and skin and breathe life into you. Then you will know that I am the Lord." (Ezekiel 37:3-6, CEV)

Dry bones. *That* is how I feel! No motivation. No muscle. No life.

And then I take a breath and fall at the throne of God. I can't do this alone. I need Him to breathe *life* into these dry bones of mine. Without Him, I am an empty soul unable to give anything to anyone . . . not my husband, not my children, not myself. I need to fall at His throne, to allow Him to help me breathe, even when my loneliness seems so consuming, even when my embarrassment and shame are overwhelming.

And He places people in my life to remind me He's there. On one pretty emotionally dark day, He sent a card in the mail from a friend. It was exactly what I needed. On the front was the penned outline of a person positioned in a yoga position called child's pose. The inscription said, "It's okay to stay in child's pose . . . for as long as you need to." Holding the card to my chest, I remember falling to the ground, sobbing tears of joy, sorrow, anger, grief, sadness, regret. My heart felt as if it had been ripped out. And there I stayed. There I prayed. There I breathed. And there *He* breathed into me.

My dear friend, someone who had herself been on an emotionally and physically taxing roller coaster, had taken the time to send me a card that she knew would mean something to me. She was one of the few who saw me in my darkest moments (because let's be honest . . . we all do a pretty good job of hiding our true selves out in public). And the vulnerability I was able to have with her opened up a world of healing for me as God used her to breathe life back into my dry bones.

I continue to keep my friend's card in my Bible as a reminder that I'm not alone. Yes, God is with me too. But this was my friend, a living, breathing person that I could hug and talk to and—despite her moving out of the country—receive support and understanding from. She helped hold me up when I could barely hold myself up, and she made sure I knew she was there. In her, God reminded me I wasn't alone.

The day I received that card was a major turning point for me. I made doctors' appointments, not for my kids but for *me*. I ordered a much-needed journal. I started something new . . . breathing, really breathing. Since then, each day, each difficult moment, each night before bed I take time to *breathe*. He gives me breath. He sustains me. I recognize that I am just dry bones if I don't focus on where my breath comes from. It is through His eyes, His breath that I can see my children in a new light and realize that attachment is a bonus in the midst of all the hard stuff. It is through His breath that I can breathe a newness of life—new every morning!

I leave you with this. First, don't let your bones get so dry that they seem unsalvageable. *Find help!* Second, as my friend did for me, take time to reach out to a friend. Your willingness to reach out, your encouragement, and also your vulnerability can make all the difference in the life of someone you know.

Finally, stay connected to the life-giving source of your breath . . . and *breathe!*

Amy Callahan

DAY 21

Religion that God our Father accepts as pure and faultless is this: to look after orphans and widows in their distress and to keep oneself from being polluted by the world.
James 1:27, NIV

If you're a Christian adoptive parent, have been involved in orphan care ministry, or even attended an Orphan Sunday, you probably have heard someone make reference to verses in the Bible about orphans. If you've only ever heard one, it was probably a reference to James 1:27.

I've seen all kinds of variations of this verse, right down to "Pure religion is to visit orphans." It is translated in the NIV, though, as, "Religion that God our Father accepts as pure and faultless is this: to look after orphans and widows in their distress and to keep oneself from being polluted by the world."

This verse was always a bit strange to me, and I can understand why people want to strip it down. So, during one of my New Testament courses in my master's program at the Ecumenical Institute of Theology in 2011, I decided I would use one of the assignments to explore this verse further. What I learned was kind of shocking to me at first, but the more I dug, the more it made sense.

Although I am no expert in biblical Greek, I had taken a few courses and was fortunate enough to have access to experts. What I found was that the English translations don't convey well what is written. There are two important places where this happens. The first is "look after," which is sometimes, and more accurately, translated as "to visit." The second, which is never translated accurately is "and to keep." The word "and" never shows up in the Greek; it is just "to keep." In fact, the meaning of the phrase is "in order to keep." I really didn't believe it at first, that there could be such a strange discrepancy in translation, but the more people I talked to, and the more I dug into James and other parts of the Bible, it really started to make sense.

So, my translation of the Greek that I think best conveys the meaning is, "Pure and undefiled worship that God the Father accepts is this: to visit orphans and widows in their distress *in order to keep* unstained by the world."

Even though times have changed in the nearly 2000 years since this was written, it is still true that there is distress among orphans and widows. The call is to go visit them, but don't think of it like a visit to the mall. We are to visit like God visits, and when God visits, He does a lot more than a simple pass-through. His visits do things like taking an entire people out of Egypt into the promised land and dying on a cross so that sins may be forgiven, as just a couple of examples. What we're called to do by visiting is to recreate those basic relationships that were broken. We are to be as a father to the fatherless and as a husband to the widow.

If you have not been involved in the lives of orphans and widows, you may not understand how this keeps you unstained by the world. However, I would be willing to bet if you have been involved in the lives of orphans and widows, that you might have a bit more insight into this. From what I have seen and experienced, even before being an adoptive parent, the experience of engaging with orphans and widows gives you an entirely new perspective on your own life and what really matters in this world. As an adoptive parent, I have experienced this, as many of us have, at a more profound level. Many of us have really been put to the test and pushed to the limits. We have experienced what the world does not understand, both in trials and what it takes to really love. So many of the stains that the world can leave us with, we no longer have. Instead, many of us have been left with the pains and stains of self-sacrifice, and so much more.

Truly visiting orphans and widows in their distress is hard. It requires self-sacrifice, self-reflection, unconditional love, and a whole lot of help from God. If you haven't experienced it, I warn you, you will be changed, you will be put to the test, and the riches and glories of this world will no longer have the same meaning for you as they might have.

However, you will experience a new, difficult, yet glorious reality, and be assured that God will accept it as pure and undefiled worship.

Patrick Corkum

_____

_____

_____

_____

_____

_____

_____

_____

_____

_____

DAY 22

. . . fixing our eyes on Jesus, the pioneer and perfecter of faith. For the joy set before him he endured the cross, scorning its shame, and sat down at the right hand of the throne of God.
Hebrews 12:2, NIV

Something has been sitting heavy in my mind over the past several days. It's the idea that if we are serving God within our giftings, it won't feel like work. It's the idea of serving in our "sweet spot." It seems to be a pretty common idea in 21st century, western Christianity. It gets me rattled and, quite honestly, angry.

Here is why.

I have to wonder if Paul was in his sweet spot when he was beaten, mobbed, and shipwrecked.

I have to wonder if Stephen was in his sweet spot when he was thrown to the ground, and stones were hurled at him.

Was Peter in his sweet spot when he was crucified upside down?

Our friends, who have fostered over ten children now and continue to serve birth families after reunification happens, were they in their sweet spot when they were investigated for child abuse because of accusations from a child who had never known safety?

What about the moms I know who are regularly spit on, scratched, hit, and raged at by the children they have chosen to love, children who lost everything imaginable before they could even walk?

Hebrews 11 is full of these stories. They knew—this great cloud of witnesses that surrounds us. They knew there was something more ahead. They believed there was something so worthy of attaining that they could throw off everything else. They understood there was wonderful joy waiting, even though trials filled the path to get there.

This place, this time—it is not our sweet spot.

The cross—the one Jesus tells us to pick up—is no sweet spot. It is life and freedom and mercy and grace. But they have been given to us at a heavy, heavy cost.

We are called to join in, to share in Christ's sufferings and carry our cross. Daily. Every single morning. **He says that *anyone* who wants to follow Him must do this.** Picking up our cross and sharing in the sufferings of Jesus will indeed feel like work—it will leave us broken and bone tired. It will reveal our weaknesses in ways that we could never have anticipated. It will draw us into stories that are too painful to imagine, let alone live.

No, the cross is no sweet spot. Our sweet spot lies ahead.

Jennifer Isaac

DAY 23

Don't urge me to leave you or to turn back from you.
Where you go I will go, and where you stay I will stay.
Your people will be my people and your God my God.
Ruth 1:16, NIV

Has your adoption journey been much more difficult than you expected? Do you feel like God has forgotten you? You may not be familiar with the small, yet powerful Old Testament book of Ruth, but it is filled with so many truths of God's faithfulness, goodness, and grace.

The book of Ruth tells us about parents—Elimelech and Naomi—and their two sons. These parents move their family from Bethlehem to the strange land of Moab. They never intended to live in Moab long. They were simply trying to escape the famine in Bethlehem. However, life is good in Moab—at least for a while. But Naomi's world comes crashing down when she experiences great loss and hardship in this strange land with the death of her husband and two sons. She becomes bitter. She believes God has made her life hard. She is left with little support in Moab at a time when a woman is completely dependent on a man's financial support. She says, "I went away [from Bethlehem] full, but the LORD has brought me back empty. Why call me Naomi? The LORD has afflicted me; the Almighty has brought misfortune upon me." (Ruth 1:20-21, NIV) In her suffering, she thinks God has forgotten her.

I think many adoptive parents can relate to Naomi. Like Naomi, you may be on a journey that often includes hardship and suffering you never expected. There is no way you can truly prepare for the adventure of adoption. Perhaps you are left with little support as your extended family and friends are not meeting your needs. You likely never expected this journey to be filled with suffering. Yet, all you can see on this adventure is hardship and destruction. And maybe you—like Naomi— wonder if God has forgotten you in your Moab. Maybe you are

90

questioning God's call or even questioning His faithfulness and goodness.

But God sends Naomi a daughter-in-law who loves and serves her. Naomi has no idea what God has in store for her through this beloved daughter-in-law, Ruth. Ruth chooses to leave everything she knows to follow Naomi. She leaves Moab—the country she grew up in. She leaves her family and her friends. She purposely gives up everything to be with Naomi. Naomi tries to encourage her to go back, but Ruth says, "Don't urge me to leave you or to turn back from you. Where you go I will go, and where you stay I will stay. Your people will be my people and your God my God." (Ruth 1:16, NIV) Ruth models God's goodness and faithfulness to Naomi.

Naomi and Ruth return to Bethlehem. It is through Ruth that God gives Naomi a guardian-redeemer: Boaz. Naomi no longer lives a life of sorrow and hardship. Boaz not only agrees to care for Naomi like a mother, but he marries Ruth. God blesses Ruth and Boaz with a son, Obed. Through God's gift of Ruth, Naomi's finds purpose for her life in caring for her grandson, Obed.

The end is nothing like Naomi originally expected. Originally, she expected to return to Bethlehem with her husband and sons. Instead, she now returns with only her daughter-in-law, Ruth. She never expected such hardship and sorrow in her life, but God had an entirely different plan for Naomi. While the journey was much harder than she envisioned, she has found joy with Obed. Even more, Naomi and Ruth's story does not end with Obed. Ruth 4:22 tells us that Obed is the father of Jesse. Jesse is the father of David through whom our Savior, Jesus Christ, comes.

God is actively working on your behalf—for your good—even before you need help. God sent Ruth to Naomi before her sons died. Naomi thought she knew what was best for Ruth and tried to send her away. But in His faithfulness, God had a plan to bring joy to Naomi through Ruth's loyalty and service.

Who has God brought into your life to walk beside you in your hardship and sorrow? Your "Ruth" may not be the person you expect, so consider who that unlikely person might be that God has sent for a greater purpose in your life. God was faithful to send Ruth to Naomi. He will be faithful to send someone to you too. God is good, and He is *always* faithful.

Prayer:

Father God, You sent Ruth to love and serve Naomi in her hardship. Lord, You know that I need a Ruth right now. Show me who You have sent into my life to love and serve me in this hard time. Help me to see their heart with Your eyes. You are faithful, and I trust You to meet my every need. In Jesus' name I pray, Amen.

Kris Kittle, Ph.D.

_____

_____

_____

_____

_____

_____

_____

_____

_____

DAY 24

For He foreordained us (destined us, planned in love for us) to be adopted (revealed) as His own children through Jesus Christ, in accordance with the purpose of His will [because it pleased Him and was His kind intent]—
Ephesians 1:5, AMPC

Maybe you're struggling with the concept of adoption today. Maybe you feel as if the plan were *yours,* and that's why everything is so hard. Maybe your life could have been easier if you hadn't decided to adopt or foster. That may be true, but may I tell you something?

"Adoption builds families the God-purposed way. Adoption is greater than or precedes the universe. Before Jesus, the Word made flesh, spoke the world into being, God chose us, planned for us to be adopted as His own, because it was His kind intent."[5]

He destined each one of us to be adopted as His own children through Jesus Christ before the foundation of the world. Before He spoke the world into being, God knew we would need a rescuer, a savior, an adoption into His family.

1. You were chosen. You were chosen to be adopted into God's family. No matter what your family history is. No matter what your parents did or didn't do. You're not a mistake. All of us have scars. Those are part of our story. God takes our wounds and weaves them into healing for ourselves and then those around us. Those purple scars you bear are not a sign of failure. They are part of your story.

2. Your children were chosen. Maybe you have foster kiddos in your home right now. They are wounded.

---

[5] Guire, Kathleen. *Positive Adoption: a Memoir.* Kathleen Guire, 2015.

Broken. Afraid. Acting out. Those attributes are a sign of something that was done to them, not who they are. They are chosen, picked out in their mother's womb, knit together. Each one of them being on the earth is not a mistake. They suffer from the sins of others or circumstances out of their control. Circumstances don't define you or them. As I say in *25 Days of Thriving Through Christmas*:[6]

"Adoption is not a second rate alternative to biological children. It's kingdom building work."

Whether a child is in your home for a week, a month, or becomes part of your forever family, you are building the kingdom. You may be planting a seed for a new way of thinking or spend years building a new foundation that says: You are loved. You are cherished. You are valuable.

3. You are anointed and qualified to raise your adopted/foster child. When we adoptive/foster parents get into the mindset that we made a mistake or didn't really hear the call to adopt/foster, we doubt. We doubt the call of God on our life. We doubt our ability. The next thing we know, everything is *too hard*. There's no grace. We begin to rely on our own natural strength and ability. It fails us. We fail us. We fail our kids. Then we get caught up in a cycle of guilt and shame. We're living in a deep dark pit. Raise your hand if you've ever felt this way (I'm raising mine).

"Truth demands confrontation, loving confrontation, but confrontation nonetheless." - Francis Schaeffer

---

[6] Guire, Kathleen. *25 Days of Thriving Through Christmas: An Advent Devotional for Adoptive and Foster Parents*. 1st ed., CreateSpace Independent Publishing Platform, 2017.

We must confront the lies and replace them with truth. If you have a child in your home through birth, foster care, or adoption, God has anointed *you* to parent them. You are qualified and equipped. When God chose you, He promised to equip you. When my four newbies first came "home," I ran on adrenaline for the first year. I was on cloud nine, excited, exhausted, and often overwhelmed from managing a household of seven kids. My stepfather, a true representative of Christ's unconditional love, died the week my four newbies arrived fresh off the plane from Poland. I was raw with anguish. My kids were raw with fear and grief. I found this set of Scriptures and copied them:

The Spirit of the Lord God is upon me, because the Lord has anointed and qualified me to preach the Gospel of good tidings to the meek, the poor, and afflicted; He has sent me to bind up and heal the brokenhearted, to proclaim liberty to the [physical and spiritual] captives and the opening of the prison and of the eyes to those who are bound,

To proclaim the acceptable year of the Lord [the year of His favor] [a]and the day of vengeance of our God, to comfort all who mourn,

To grant [consolation and joy] to those who mourn in Zion—to give them an ornament (a garland or diadem) of beauty instead of ashes, the oil of joy instead of mourning, the garment [expressive] of praise instead of a heavy, burdened, and failing spirit—that they may be called oaks of righteousness [lofty, strong, and magnificent, distinguished for uprightness, justice, and right standing with God], the planting of the Lord, that He may be glorified. (Isaiah 61:1-3, AMPC)

These Scriptures became my purpose. They backed me up when I didn't feel called or chosen. I recited them. Wrote them. Picked them apart. Anointed. Qualified. Good tidings. My kids were meek, poor, and afflicted. They had broken hearts, and so did I.

You may be in a similar situation. Maybe you are in the middle of your own Job syndrome, and you don't know if you are called anymore. But your calling didn't wear off! It just need a bit of stirring up. Read those verses again, and put your name in them. Recite them as proclamations over you and your children. Confront the lies. Remember the truths from the word of God. Write the truths on paper, and pray they are written on your heart and the hearts of your children. You were chosen. You kids were chosen. God has anointed and qualified you.

Kathleen Guire

DAY 25

Friends, when life gets really difficult, don't jump to the conclusion that God isn't on the job. Instead, be glad that you are in the very thick of what Christ experienced. This is a spiritual refining process, with glory just around the corner.
1 Peter 4:12-13, MSG

Adoption built my faith and my family.

As I became a momma in this way I didn't expect, I prayed for God to use our story to encourage others. While we were navigating the adoption process the first two times, I knew hardly anyone who had adopted or was adopted. Now, a momma of three kids who came to us through private, domestic adoptions, I also have a community of moms who understand.

This online community is the answer to my prayers. Yes, it's one of the ways God is using our story, like I prayed for, but it's also been a blessing to me as I navigate parenting. Within this community, I've often quoted 1 Peter 4:13 from The Message: "This is a spiritual refining process, with glory just around the corner."

Regardless of where people are in the process, I want these other moms to remember we're in these adoptions and this life together. And the glory really is coming. This online community has been a safe space where we share prayer requests, resources, and updates. Some of us get to gather around real-life tables for lunches and watch our kids befriend one another.

My husband and I started thinking about adoption in the fall of 2006, and my oldest daughter was born less than nine months later. We adopted our son in 2009 and then our youngest daughter in 2015. I may have known more about adoption each time, but it all was—and still is in the trenches of parenting—a spiritual refining process.

Having a community of people who have been where you are or are going where you've been reminds me of God's faithfulness and provides an outlet for moms to support one another. My community gradually formed through conversations with other moms, and then I launched a Facebook group not long before my youngest was born.

Adoption involves piles of paperwork, much wait time on matches and responses, relationships with biological families or the absence of biological information, choices another woman makes that directly affect the child, conversations to help children understand identity and purpose, and possible therapies to undo trauma or heal physical ailments. There are steps you can take and documents you can sign, but the whole process is about surrendering and trusting. While common themes run through each adoption, every process getting to actually growing a family is different.

And sometimes, that's hard.

Sometimes, it's hard to see God in those details because adoption is always rooted in brokenness. Yes, God makes beauty from ashes, but sometimes it takes a while to see even pieces of that because we won't see the full picture until heaven.

Adoption requires people to believe in a miracle before they see it, asks people to embrace brokenness with a still-coming promise of redemption, and offers an up-close glimpse of what the gospel is really about.

We have an inheritance and forever family because God adopts us. Just like my kids share our last name, God calls us his own. We welcomed these three kids into the responsibilities and privileges of being in a family; God welcomes us into his home. Yes, there are glimpses of his kingdom here on earth and through adoption processes, but there's also a promise of the eternal home Jesus is preparing for us and the children we get to lead to him. This is the God who is working for us during earthly adoptions too.

Through our adoptions, God demonstrated to me that He is continually near. He's in the details because He is working for us, with us, and through us. These earthly adoption stories become His glory—and that's even easier to notice when we have a community with which to share it.

Hang on, the glory really is coming—even if it doesn't look like you expect.

Kristin Hill Taylor

_____

_____

_____

_____

_____

_____

_____

_____

_____

_____

_____

_____

DAY 26

The hearts of the people CRY OUT to the Lord...let your
tears flow like a river day and night; give yourself no
relief, your eyes no rest. Arise, CRY OUT in the
night...POUR OUT your heart like water in the presence
of the Lord; LIFT UP your hands to Him for the lives of
your children who faint from hunger at the
head of every street.
Lamentations 2:18-19, NIV

If you didn't get the chance to know Kalkidan you missed an amazing young girl with a smile that would light up a room and melt your heart. She also had a tender heart of gold and a larger-than-life personality. Having lost both of her parents to AIDS, she was adopted by our dear friends from an orphanage in Ethiopia. Sadly, in 2014, at the age of thirteen, Kalkidan was killed in a tragic car accident.

Even though, in this life, she was surrounded by an incredible family and countless friends who showered her with love and encouragement, she was just beginning to figure out how to accept it. As often is the case with children who have suffered trauma, neglect, and abuse, it is not easy for them to understand the unconditional love of a family or a God who loves without strings. They don't always see themselves the way we see them, let alone how God sees them.

I know that in heaven, Kalkidan now fully understands this, and I suspect that her smile is even more magical. I would venture to say that everyone who had the privilege of loving Kalkidan also learned an invaluable lesson about unconditional love. Not surprisingly, the student became the teacher, and we are all better at both giving and receiving love for having loved Kalkidan.

While my family's tears upon hearing of her death could have filled a bucket, and over a thousand friends and family attended her memorial service, there are many like Kalkidan whose passing will mostly go unnoticed. I suspect that would have been the case had she remained in the orphanage. The world is full of Kalkidans who need the constant assurance that their life matters and that regardless of anything they do or don't do, they are loved.

I am convinced that everyone needs a Kalkidan in their life to teach them this lesson. I hope you will look for one in your life. They don't just reside in orphanages in Ethiopia. They are in every homeless shelter, prison, and foster care agency. They are also in every school, church, and family.

These are children who, as a result of their brokenness, don't always behave the way we would prefer and whose beauty and gifts will oftentimes go unnoticed unless someone is there to walk alongside them. Don't sit back and criticize and judge them; get off your high horse and show them the unconditional love God has shown you. Find a Kalkidan, and you will never be the same.

Dan Hamer

_____

_____

_____

_____

_____

_____

_____

DAY 27

For this reason, since the day we heard about you, we have not stopped praying for you. We continually ask God to fill you with the knowledge of his will through all the wisdom and understanding that the Spirit gives, so that you may live a life worthy of the Lord and please him in every way: bearing fruit in every good work, growing in the knowledge of God, being strengthened with all power according to his glorious might so that you may have great endurance and patience, and giving joyful thanks to the Father, who has qualified you to share in the inheritance of his holy people in the kingdom of light.
Colossians 1:9-12, NIV

One of my kiddos faces some lifelong health challenges—the results of a birth defect that silenced the delivery room at his arrival, requiring three major surgeries within days of delivery. Other surgeries have followed. He is a teenager now but still requires frequent visits to the children's hospital for painful procedures and additional surgeries.

As he got older, I watched his childlike faith . . . and the faith of his mother . . . challenged by the well-meaning but cliché prayers we were praying with him. All of a sudden, the prayers that once sufficed felt increasingly toxic. The "rescue" we sought was not coming. "Healing" for his defect was something he likely will not see this side of heaven. And often . . . things did not go well. Surgery failures. Complications. Painful setbacks. Prolonged hospitalizations. In the recesses of my quiet thoughts, I felt like my prayers were not working. Perhaps I was doing something wrong? Either that, or God simply wasn't listening. Had He abandoned us? Logically, it seemed, it had to be one of those. I can only imagine my young son's quiet thoughts and fears as we prayed these apparently ineffective prayers with him.

Then I read a blog post by Bronwyn Lea that changed the way we prayed. Bronwyn suggested we change our "Make it better" prayers to "Make it count." [7]

This simple shift in language and expectation brought new light. The next time we checked in for surgery, I took my son's hand, and we honestly and fervently prayed, "OK. God. Darn it. If we must do this again, then we need You to make this count. Please. Make us kinder. Make us stronger. Make us more compassionate and more courageous. Bring nearness. And bravery. And gentleness. To a degree we knew not of before. Jesus, make this count. Please."

With these prayers, we found new life in our relationship to the God of our prayers. Prayers often do not set us free from the hardness of life. Sometimes, rescue doesn't come as we sit in suffering with our loved ones. Could it be that even in the difficulties and apparent silence, God was still working? When we prayed, "Make it Count," we found Him present. We found Him moving in our lives even when circumstances did not change.

Now, I don't think this solves the mystery of God's sovereignty nor replaces those prayers for healing and help we should keep praying. Questions about prayer have endured through the ages. I don't have answers. I just know that my prayers *may* or *may not* alter my circumstances. But they can, however, always be used to align my heart to what pleases Him. And well, that gives me hope. That gives me strength and the grace to face another day. We can make it count. We can trust and believe and call out to Him . . . that whatever may come, He can make it count in our lives.

---

[7] Lea, Bronwyn. "One Little Word That Radically Changed My Prayers," Bronwyn Lea (blog), August 6, 2013, https://bronlea.com/2013/08/06/one-little-word-that-radically-changed-my-prayers/.

I imagine most of us have faced something personally or with our kids that feels like our heart's cry is falling on deaf ears and the idle hands of rescue.

If you find yourself there today, ashamed to say it out loud, you can know I am praying with you. I am praying the only way I know how in those moments. "Make it count, God. Please."

I sometimes use this prayer from Henri Nouwen to reinforce these words when I can't find my own:

Dear Lord, in the midst of much inner turmoil and restlessness, there is a consoling thought; maybe you are working in me in a way I cannot yet feel or experience or understand. My mind is not able to concentrate on you, my heart is not able to remain centered, and it seems as if you are absent and have left me alone. But in faith, I cling to you. I believe your Spirit reaches deeper and further than my mind or heart, and that profound movements are not the first to be noticed.

Therefore, Lord, I promise I will not turn away, not give up, not stop praying, even when it seems useless, pointless, and a waste of time and effort. I want to let you know that I love you even though I do not feel loved by you, and that I hope in you even though I often experience despair. Let this be a little dying I can do with you and for you as a way of experiencing some solidarity with the millions in this world who suffer far more than I do. Amen.[8]

Jody Landers

---

[8] Nouwen, Henri J. M. "Thursday, May 10." *In A Cry for Mercy: Prayers from the Genessee.* New York: Doubleday, 1981.

DAY 28

Therefore, my dear brothers and sisters, stand firm. Let
nothing move you. Always give yourselves fully to the
work of the Lord, because you know that your labor in
the Lord is not in vain.
1 Corinthians 15:58, NIV

I recently talked with a mom of two young children adopted from foster care. With grown kids and now in her early fifties, she and her husband didn't go into foster care hoping to adopt, but they loved these kids. When it became clear the children couldn't return to their original family, these empty nesters said, "Yes," to being a forever family.

And you know what? It's beautiful.

And it's really hard.

Research tells us trauma shapes the brain and interrupts normal development. We know healing the brain takes far more than love, although that's essential. It takes time and often intense therapeutic parenting. This healing commonly requires help from a team of professionals. And it's long—loving kids from "hard places" is a long journey.

Adoption looks messy, especially to people outside our families who don't understand our kids' unique needs. In fact, it looks and feels messy to those of us on the inside too, but we're no longer surprised. It's become our lives.

This mom told me people have questioned whether they made the right decision. Did they really hear God? After all, this appears to be a bit of train wreck.

My response? The folks asking those questions need to read the Bible. Time and again in scripture, we see people follow God with all their hearts and yet suffer. Hardship is their companion.

There are so many examples, but today, the apostle Paul comes to mind. He was beaten, stoned, shipwrecked, imprisoned, sleepless, hungry, and thirsty. Following Jesus did not make his life easy. It cost him everything.

As my pastor says, **"There is a cost to being used by God."**

You cannot enter into a child's suffering without suffering in some way too. Trauma is messy and spills over onto the ones willing to come near. Yet you have immersed yourself in it in the name of love.

Foster and adoptive parents, you are being used by God. You are a shelter for children needing to know they are precious, valued, and loved. When they look in your eyes and see warmth and acceptance, they begin to trust you, which is foundational for healing.

I know many of you face hardships as a result of saying, "Yes," to caring for vulnerable children. Don't lose heart; hold on.

The apostle Paul said it himself, **"Your labor is not in vain."**

You are good parents, doing good work in hard circumstances. God sees you and is near.

Lisa Qualls

_____

_____

_____

_____

_____

_____

DAY 29

Let the words of my mouth and the meditation of my heart be acceptable in Your sight, O Lord, my strength and my Redeemer.
Psalm 19:14, NKJV

It's easy to get caught up in the things we're supposed to do. Overwhelm often comes from the demands on our time, energy, and resources as parents of kids who have experienced trauma. Most of us, at some point, have felt the pull to do, or be, "better"—whatever that may look like in our individual lives, and our families. As people who love our people, there's an innate desire to keep improving the way we demonstrate that love.

I've heard this verse many times over the years, specifically the opening phrasing that reminds us to keep our words and thoughts holy. But not long ago, I came across it while I was reading, and I couldn't move on. It felt heavy to me that day because we had been experiencing a peak trauma time and behaviors had been intense. I knew I had failed to keep the words of my mouth and meditations of my heart acceptable before God. Momentarily, it was shame that settled in my spirit as I reflected on the Scripture. Weariness had circumvented my peace and joy, and it showed in my words and meditations.

I re-read the verse, fully aware that shame is never the Holy Spirit's way of guiding us. It was then that the final phrasing of the verse jumped out at me: *my strength and my Redeemer.*

Weariness often comes when we forget that God is our strength. We strive to find our ability within ourselves. We measure our success by accomplishing our to-do lists. We read the books and blogs and manuals, implementing the latest parenting techniques. We toil and spin, determined to do whatever we can to help our child(ren) and family. Ultimately, we sometimes fail to make our requests known to God with thanksgiving, so that His peace can guard our hearts and minds. (Philippians 4:6)

It is not left to us to muster the tenacity to walk this journey. God did not marvel at our capabilities before asking us to say "yes" to loving and parenting children who have experienced deep loss. Instead, He declares that He, in all His perfection, is our strength. (Psalm 46:1)

He is also our Redeemer. He, alone, has the power to redeem our insecurities and weaknesses so that we can be the parents He desires us to be. He redeems the brokenness of our pasts so that we can walk through healing with our child(ren).

Our enemy, Satan, is a master manipulator. One of his key strategies is to take a blessing from God and, through deception, cause us to view it as a burden. So many times, the heart of compassion God has given us for our children becomes a wearisome burden because we forget the beautiful truth that God, alone, is our child(ren)'s strength and Redeemer! We must avoid the temptation to attempt carrying the burden of our child(ren)'s past. That is not God's answer or design. Rather, we have the honor and privilege of showing them the way to the Savior, so that He can carry both of us through grief and loss.

You see, when we understand the power of God's rightful place as strength and Redeemer, we free ourselves from unrealistic expectations. We can come boldly before His throne of grace in times of need. (Hebrews 4:16) When our physical, emotional, mental, or spiritual stamina is running low, we can surrender to Himinstead of striving. There is freedom from the need to control and fix—because it was never our job in the first place!

The freedom we find in allowing God to do His part, as we do ours, has a trickle effect to our child(ren). We demonstrate to them the critical principles of coming humbly but boldly to God; admitting our need and allowing Him to meet it; and finding our identity in who He says we are. For children who have suffered trauma, grief, and loss, these are imperative lessons in felt safety, trust, and acceptance.

Let the words of my mouth and the meditation of my heart be acceptable in Your sight, O Lord, my strength and my Redeemer. (Psalm 19:14, NKJV)

Let those words sink in. Dwell on them. Ask the Holy Spirit to show you what they mean to you today, and how you can allow God His rightful position as your strength and Redeemer!

Naomi Quick

_____

_____

_____

_____

_____

_____

_____

_____

_____

_____

DAY 30

Whatever you do, work at it with all your heart, as working for the Lord, not for human masters, since you know that you will receive an inheritance from the Lord as a reward. It is the Lord Christ you are serving.
Colossians 3:23-24, NIV

Luke's gospel tells of the Angel Gabriel appearing to Mary, Mary conceiving the Christ child by the power of the Holy Spirit, Mary's visit to Elizabeth, Mary's song of praise to the Lord, the lowly manger birth, and even angels appearing to shepherds in the fields.

But look more closely. Luke's gospel barely mentions an important character in this story. While God gets God's deserved credit and Mary executes her lines poetically and role with servant mastery, and while Elizabeth is there to offer assurance and support, another character is off in the shadows. A character who, upon learning of Mary's pregnancy outside of marital relations, literally held her life and the life of her unborn child in his hands. Infidelity, after all, could warrant death according to Jewish law, and at the very least, divorce. Yet, that isn't what happens.

Where is Joseph as this all plays out? What is he thinking? Did he seek anyone for counsel? Luke's gospel mentions Joseph only passively and for lineage sake and never gives an account of Joseph's own thoughts or words. In fact, there is no record of Joseph saying anything at all, not one word of his own, in all of Scripture. Joseph only gets fourteen mentions in the entire Bible. For a character who plays a pivotal role in the birth and childrearing of Jesus, Joseph really doesn't get much ink cred, does he? We have no idea what happens to him after Jesus' teen years either, as scripture doesn't tell us.

Matthew's gospel account is really the only place where we get to know a little bit about Joseph, and even there we don't learn much. What we do learn, however, is that Joseph is a righteous man, and that his quiet, humble obedience to the Lord played a major role in God's redemptive plans. Despite what I imagine to be Joseph's own fear and shame—who, after all, would believe their Holy Spirit conception story—he obeys the Lord.

Lucky for you and I, to the best of my knowledge, none have been asked by God to be the mother of Jesus's second coming. Lucky for us, none have had to tell our spouses that we are pregnant with God's child. Lucky for us, God is still God, Jesus already accomplished God's purposes, and we are safe with the promises of our Lord, despite all of the hurt and hurting around us.

As adoptive parents, however, we may be able to relate to Joseph's shadowy role in the life of a child. We may be able to relate to being sidelined, to living with fear, uncertainty, and shame even, while trying our best to be faithful to the call God has placed on our lives. We may be able to relate to the immense responsibility that comes with raising children who are born not of our blood. We may be able to relate to working tirelessly day in and day out to love, raise, and protect a child whose life inevitably brings us heartache and pain, intermixed with joy and purpose.

In addition, raising children with histories of trauma can be especially lonely and isolating, devastating even. *Does anyone see how scared we are? How tired? Does anyone see the cost? Positively, does anyone realize how transformative this path is? Will others be willing to assume the risk to experience the reward? Even if it means they get no mention, no credit?* For sure, raising children who have endured multiple traumas is *the* most difficult vocation God has called me to, and also the most rewarding. Like Joseph, our own identity and the significant role we play as parents may get overshadowed or confused, threatened and belittled even, as God calls us back into the ring each day to support, give care, provide, encourage, raise up, and empower our children.

God has placed an amazing and powerful call on our lives, but one that seldom gets accolades, and a call that has the worst road map ever, as we must constantly change and adapt along the way. We are still people, men and women, who exist apart from our role as adoptive and foster parents, and yet our identity has also been permanently altered due to the call God has placed on our lives. Like Joseph's response to God when the Angel appeared to him in a dream (Matthew 1:20), when we said yes to God's call on our lives, we did so in faith and obedience, despite not knowing where the path would take us.

For many, the path has taken us on long and windy roads filled with great joy and, also, great pain. The path has taken us to counseling, hospitals, doctor's offices, school board meetings, principal's offices, championship soccer tournaments, art shows, concerts, and college admission offices, not to mention probation offices. The path has shown us God in ways many of us may never have wanted to know God. The path has shown us the world's brokenness, systemic injustices, and corruption of power in ways many of us would rather have remained ignorant to.

And yet, here we stand. Bruised, scarred, often confused and lonely, and yet capable of a bigger love than we likely ever imagined. Here we stand, or sit, or lie, often in the shadows, like Joseph, but most definitely changed in significant ways from the day of our first yes.

What I admire most about Joseph in our loud and "see me, me, me" world, is that in his humility and pure obedience, he refuses to allow his individual experience to overshadow the collective experience God is birthing. He doesn't allow the "I" to overpower the "we." Joseph does not ask to be tagged, shared, or mentioned. He doesn't ask us to buy his latest book or subscribe to his latest leadership podcast: leading while scared. He doesn't launch a new kind of ministry for parents of children conceived by the Holy Spirit.

Rather, Joseph humbly, quietly accepts the call God has placed on his life. He reminds me that we need each other and that no matter how lonely the adoptive, foster, and/or trauma road gets, we weren't meant to do it alone *or* do it for praise. He reminds me, reminds *us*, that whatever we are doing, if we are doing it out of our love for God and love for the other, we are doing enough.

We *are* enough. No platform needed. No accolades. No mentions. But please, just a little more sleep. And perhaps a few less rages. And maybe, just maybe, a trauma-informed world. Come, Lord Jesus . . .

Monica Reynolds

CONTRIBUTORS

Kristin Berry

Day 17

Kristin Berry is an author, blogger and public speaker. She and her husband Mike are the proud parents of eight children, in-laws to two sons-in-law and grandparents of three. They live on a small farm in Indiana and can be found caring for a variety of cute but fairly useless farm animals.

https://confessionsofanadoptiveparent.com

Mike Berry

Day 11

Mike Berry is the cofounder, along with his wife, Kristin, of the award-winning parenting blog *Confessions of an Adoptive Parent* and the support and resource site Oasis Community. He is a featured writer and influencer for Disney website Babble.com, and his work has also been featured on Yahoo Parenting, The Good Men Project, *The Huffington Post*, RightNow Media, Michael Hyatt's Platform University, and goinswriter.com. A sought-after speaker, he travels across the U.S. extensively throughout the year to camps, retreats, and conferences. Before becoming a full-time author and speaker, he spent 17 years in family life ministry in churches in Ohio and Indiana. He lives in Indianapolis, Indiana, with his wife and their eight children.

https://confessionsofanadoptiveparent.com

Tara Bradford

Day 7

Tara Bradford was born in South Korea and then adopted in 1971. She grew up in North Dakota where she met her husband of 25 years. They had two children biologically and then grew their family through adoption of a sibling group of three kids from Ethiopia. Tara is the Founder of FACES, a nonprofit providing support to adoptive and foster families in Montana.

Amy J. Callahan
Day 20

Amy Callahan is a recovering judgmental, people-pleasing Christian. Really. (She's all about cutting to the chase.) A former missionary and teacher in Asia, always an advocate for the vulnerable and the oppressed, and a budding author, she is currently trying to figure out what in the world her Enneagram number could be. Born in Boston, raised on the sandy shores of Clearwater, Florida, then on to more beaches in SE Asia and now sitting by a fire or falling down the ski slopes in Idaho, Amy is married to Kimmer Callahan and mom to four pretty incredible kids (bragging rights). They started their adoption journey in 2008 in China and finished there in 2016 with the adoption of two older children.

Melissa Corkum
Day 8

Melissa Corkum is a parent and wellness coach helping parents find calm and confidence through mindful parenting and essential oils. She is an adult adoptee and married to Patrick. They live in Maryland, are parents to six kids by birth and adoption, and grandparents to an adorable granddaughter. She writes at The Cork Board and is the co-founder of The Adoption Connection (www.theadoptionconnection.com), a resource/coaching site and podcast for adoptive and foster families.
http://thecorkboardonline.com

Patrick Corkum
Day 21

Patrick Corkum is married to Melissa, and they have six children and one granddaughter. He has a Master of Arts in Theology from the Ecumenical Institute of Theology in Baltimore, Maryland. His passion for loving God through visiting orphans and widows has spurred him to be involved in many related ministries including adopting four children.

Jen Decker
Day 19

Jen Decker wears many hats . . . wife, mom, friend, sister and most importantly daughter of the King! Growing up in an isolated adoptive family in the church has given her a heart for supporting foster and adoptive parents on their journey. She is the director of Network 1.27 Foster Adoption Ministry at Westside Family Church in Lenexa, Kansas where she learns through her mistakes on the regular and where a gracious God keeps making all things new!

Jamie C. Finn
Day 1

Jamie C. Finn is the biological, adoptive, and foster mother of 4-6 children. When she's not homeschooling, changing diapers, playing Pokemon, making slime, and singing "Let it Go," she spends her time encouraging, equipping, and serving foster and adoptive parents. She is the author of Foster the Family Blog and the host of the Real Mom Podcast. Jamie serves as the director of Foster the Family, a nonprofit which seeks to encourage and support foster and adoptive families, mobilize the church and community for foster care and adoption, and advocate for vulnerable children.

http://www.fosterthefamilyblog.com

Kathleen Guire
Day 24

Kathleen Guire is an adoptive parent of four, mother of seven and grandmother of nine. She has led numerous education and support groups. Kathleen has written *Positive Adoption: A Memoir* chronicling her childhood story intertwined with the story of the adoption of her children. She has also written *Five Things: A Tiny Handbook for Adoptive/Foster Families*, and *25 Days of Thriving Through Christmas: An Advent Devotional,* and two novels. Kathleen is a certified Empowered to Connect Parent Trainer. Kathleen runs a website and ministry "The Whole House."

https://thewholehouse.org

Dan Hamer

Day 26

Dan Hamer has served as the Senior Associate Pastor at Overlake Christian Church in Redmond, Washington since June 2009. During his time there he and his wife, Kathleen launched the Vulnerable Children Ministry which has been responsible for creating programs supporting foster care, adoption, vulnerable children, and street children both locally and globally. Dan is a Certified Public Accountant and holds a B.A. from Anderson University (Indiana) and did graduate work at the University of Southern California in the Masters of Business Taxation program. He has a long history of caring for at risk children and is father to five children, two of whom joined his family via international adoption.

Kathleen Hamer

Day 3

Kathleen Hamer has worked with at risk and homeless youth for many years. She is a youth outreach counselor at Overlake Christian Church in Redmond, WA where she and her husband Dan began the Orphan Care Initiative in 2009. Kathleen earned her undergraduate degree at California State University at Long Beach and her Masters in Marriage, Family and Child Counseling from Azusa Pacific University. Kathleen is the mother of five children, two who joined their family through international adoption and grandmother to three darling granddaughters.

Maria Hansen-Quine

Day 15

Maria Hansen-Quine, LASW, CSC, considers herself to be a precious jewels mamma, as she passionately believes that each one of her children is a gift from her Heavenly Father. Maria and her husband Sam (an adult adoptee) have nine precious jewels, seven through adoption and two born biologically. Maria so believes in the value of children that she's devoted the past 22 years to working with jewels from hard places. Maria currently works as an inner city school counselor.

http://preciousjewelsmamma.blogspot.com

Jennifer Isaac

Day 22

Jennifer Isaac has spent much of the last decade parenting and advocating in the areas of foster care as well as medical needs adoption. She lives in Denver with her husband, Greg, and has four children - born in four countries (ages 15 to 20). She works at Bridges to Prosperity and when not working or navigating the tricky waters of parenting teens, she loves hiking, camping, snowshoeing, and teaching group fitness classes at her local YMCA.

Kris Kittle

Day 23

Kris Kittle, PhD, and her husband have been married over 20 years. They have two children through adoption. She earned her PhD from the University of North Texas. She currently teaches leadership communication as an adjunct professor at a private, Christian university. Dr. Kittle is coauthor of *Wisdom from Adoptive Families: Joys and Challenges of Older Child Adoption*. She blogs at AdoptionSurvival.com and KrisKittle.com.

http://adoptionsurvival.com

Jody Landers
Day 27

Jody Landers lives with her family in Olympia, WA. She is the mom of six, including twins adopted from Sierra Leone. At the present day, all six kids are teenagers which means she does not currently have the capacity to write bios. The end.

Brandi Lea
Day 5

Brandi Lea is a single mama of three, living and loving life in the mountains of Colorado. Through the adventures and misadventures of African adoption, divorce and parenting children of trauma, Brandi has developed a passion for healing that starts with ourselves and extends throughout the world. She is the founder of Beauty For Ashes Worldwide. Their two projects include Beauty for Ashes Uganda (working toward sustainable development and deep healing for 1,200 single mamas and widows in rural Uganda) and SoulCare (providing retreats and a sisterhood of understanding for nonprofit leaders doing hard and holy work around the world).

Stacy Manning
Day 6

Stacy Manning, RN, mom of six kids (three adopted & three bio) and full-time grandmother of one, is on a mission to help adoptive and foster parents get their families to Happy & Healthy. Through her book, *Adoptive Parent Intentional Parent*, her Facebook community Adoptive and Foster Parenting, and her Intentional Parent Coaching Group she is empowering thousands of families with tools and support. In addition, she hosts a second Facebook community, Trauma-Sensitive Teachers, and has launched Impact a program to help create trauma sensitive classrooms across the country.

https://www.tohavehope.com

Tereasa M. Mansfield
Day 18

Tereasa Mansfield is a parent trainer and coach who helps overwhelmed moms understand disruptive behaviors, connect with their children, and lower stress so they can feel joy in parenting and hope for the future.

http://tereasamansfield.com

Ed & Bev McDowell
Day 16

Ed and Bev McDowell live in Stanwood, WA. Adoption and care of children have been central to their personal and professional lives, as they seek to share the powerful love of Christ to as many people as they possibly can.

https://www.standpoint360.com

Nicole Pritchard
Day 13

Nicole Pritchard is the parent of four sons through both birth and foster care adoption. She blogs over at Coffee Colored Sofa where she shares how parenting is changing her.

http://www.coffeecoloredsofa.com

Lisa Qualls
Day 28

Lisa Qualls is married to Russ and the mom of twelve kids by birth and adoption (and sometimes more through foster care). Lisa is a TBRI practitioner and the co-author, together with the late Dr. Karyn Purvis, of a new book (2020) for parents of children from "hard places." She writes the blog One Thankful Mom and is the co-founder of The Adoption Connection (www.theadoptionconnection.com), a resource/coaching site and award-winning podcast for adoptive and foster families.

http://www.onethankfulmom.com

Naomi Quick

Day 29

Naomi Quick loves Jesus. She is married to her best friend, John. They have six amazing, beautiful kids, two of whom have been adopted from the foster care system. Naomi homeschools their tribe of world changers. She is a type-A, list-making, change-fearing girl living an adventure that demands flexibility, spontaneity, and constant change! She writes over at Living Out 127. Through her words, she prays you'll find something that points your heart to the Dream Giver and the Author of each of our stories – Jesus.

https://www.127living.com

Bev Regier

Day 12

Bev Regier is an adoptive and birth mom to seven adult children and grandmother to four. She and her husband, Chuck, farm in Kansas, raising crops and antibiotic-free, hormone-free hogs. Besides writing, she enjoys knitting, reading, movies, podcasts and spending time with friends and family. They are active in their local church.

Monica Reynolds

Day 30

Monica Reynolds is a wife, mother of five, and United Methodist clergywoman serving in the Washington DC metro area. In addition to serving as a local church pastor, Monica is passionate about advocating for trauma informed education and practices, and is a proponent of the missional church movement in our day and time. Adoption has stolen and broken her heart again and again. She writes irregularly at Emerging Mama and hosts the Collared Chicks podcasts.

http://emergingmama.com

Jeff and Jen Summers

Day 2

Jeff Summers is a pastor, writer, speaker, devoted husband and father. He and his wife Jen love to encourage and equip other adoptive parents through coaching and spiritual counseling, online or in person. They currently have ten children, seven of whom are teenagers!

http://adoptivedadsunite.com

Kristin Hill Taylor

Day 25

Kristin Hill Taylor believes in seeking God as the author of every story and loves swapping these stories with friends on her porch. She has a bachelor's in print journalism from Murray State University and worked in various newsrooms before she became a stay-at-home mom. She volunteers and does projects that involve writing, promoting, organizing, and hosting. She lives in Murray, Kentucky, with her family.

https://kristinhilltaylor.com

Jen Tompkins

Day 10

Jen Tompkins loves to encourage people, especially women, to love God more deeply by exploring His Word with passion and excitement, and maybe a little humor. She serves as Director of Women's Ministry at Morning Star Church in Salem, OR. Jen's favorite role is wife to Trent and mama of three: a spunky blonde, a sassy redhead, and a charming little Southeast Asian who joined their family through adoption in 2012.

Rebecca Vahle

Day 9

Rebecca Vahle is the Founder and Director of Training and Curriculum Development for the Family to Family Support Network (FFSN), a pro-education, non-profit organization.

FFSN began as the Family to Family Adoption Support
Network Program at Parker Adventist Hospital in Parker,
Colorado in 2004. The program, created by Rebecca, was the
first hospital-based adoption support program in the nation and
has been recognized as defining best practice in handling the
complex, emotional and logistical needs present in infant
adoptions in the hospital setting.

In 2015, FFSN was created to share and expand the program
and care model into hospitals nationwide with the goal of
educating healthcare professionals on the complexities of
serving all unique families and empowering hospitals to be a hub
of resources to connect families early in pregnancy with needed
community resources. Rebecca has a masters degree in
education, was a parenting instructor with Centura Health for 17
years, and is the mother to three amazing teens who came home
through infant adoption.

https://www.familytofamilysupport.org

Mark Vatsaas
Day 14

Mark Vatsaas is a TBRI Practitioner, parenting coach, trainer,
speaker, the father of six astounding kids, and the husband of an
extraordinary wife and mother. Mark is a fierce advocate for
children and the families that care for them, supporting families
world-wide through his coaching and as a moderator of the
15,000 strong Facebook group, Parenting with Connection.

http://seenandheard.coach

Wendy Willard
Day 4

Wendy Willard and her husband have been privileged to share
their lives with a lot of different people over the past 20 years.
They had two daughters by birth and also fostered 18 other kids.
Then they started an adoption care ministry in Central America
to house and support families traveling to complete the

adoption process in Nicaragua. At least 24 adopting families lived with the Willards, each for three to eight months at a time. They've also hosted international exchange students, missionaries, and whomever else God brings into their home. They love the adventure of following God wherever he leads.

http://www.stillnotthereyet.com

the ADOPTION
connection

Being an adoptive parent can be overwhelming and lonely.
We provide post adoption resources and friends who
understand. You will gain confidence in your parenting and
hope for your family's future.

We offer hope, share wisdom, and mentor you along the
way. You are not alone.

Download free resources and listen to our award-winning
podcast at www.theadoptionconnection.com.

for **foster & adoptive parents**

WE UNDERSTAND what it's like to raise kids who come from traumatic pasts. We know firsthand what it's like to make the sacrifices. To be weighed down with shame and sheer exhaustion. We know. **WE ARE RIGHT THERE WITH YOU**. That's why we started Refresh back in 2011.

Some people say Refresh shouldn't be called a conference because it really is more of an experience. And you know what? They might be right. So, call it whatever you want, but **JUST COME AND CHECK IT OUT**.

www.therefreshconference.org

37911031R00080

Made in the USA
Middletown, DE
04 March 2019